ETA 2 Oneness

ALSO BY ROBIN L. JOHNSON

Awakening of a Chocolate Mystic
by Balboa Press in 2011

ETA 2 Oneness

A Journey to Spiritual Awakening

Robin L. Johnson

BALBOA.
PRESS

A DIVISION OF HAY HOUSE

Balboa Press books may be ordered through booksellers or by contacting:

Balboa Press
A Division of Hay House
1663 Liberty Drive
Bloomington, IN 47403
www.balboapress.com
1 (877) 407-4847

Because of the dynamic nature of the Internet, any web addresses or
links contained in this book may have changed since publication and
may no longer be valid. The views expressed in this work are solely those
of the author and do not necessarily reflect the views of the publisher,
and the publisher hereby disclaims any responsibility for them.

The author of this book does not dispense medical advice or prescribe the use
of any technique as a form of treatment for physical, emotional, or medical
problems without the advice of a physician, either directly or indirectly. The
intent of the author is only to offer information of a general nature to help
you in your quest for emotional and spiritual well-being. In the event you use
any of the information in this book for yourself, which is your constitutional
right, the author and the publisher assume no responsibility for your actions.

The cover photo was taken in Africa by the author
Robin L. Johnson while sailing on the Zambezi River in Zimbabwe.

Printed in the United States of America.

ISBN: 978-1-4525-1930-2 (sc)
ISBN: 978-1-4525-1931-9 (e)

Library of Congress Control Number: 2014914122

Balboa Press rev. date: 08/04/2014

In loving memory of my friend and mentor Debbie Ford, New York Times Best Selling Author, who taught me through life coaching concepts how to "own all of who I am, especially my shadow"

"Judgment always distorts your perception because it separates reality based upon changeable scales of desire..."

Contents

Foreword

I just loved reading Robin's insights and life's lessons. She freely shares easy to follow concepts that will reframe perspectives of old experiences, if you allow her to do it with her wordsmith craft. This is the second of Robin's books that I have had the pleasure to learn from. This message is one of heart. Every person who embarks on the "road less travelled" is truly motivated by a deep desire to do so. The commitment to self to seek one's connection to God source is the biggest one we will ever make, much bigger than signing a marriage contract, buying a house or having a baby.

Robin's commitment to God clearly shows in her actions not just her words. What makes her special is that she did not choose this path because circumstances and pain compelled her to seek out an answer; the conscious choice was motivated when she moved as far up the ladder of self-realization and success as it could take her yet she still felt unfulfilled.

Allow me to introduce this expressive wise woman to you: I first met Robin in Peru as I arrived there as part of a workshop with Gregg Braden. Being South African and more reserved by nature, I was surprised when Robin sat down next to me in the computer room and started talking to me as we both finished checking email. We had an instant connection and from that point on many deep discussions about the evolution of humanity through spiritual eyes. Not only did we talk extensively in Peru, but I had the pleasure of hosting Robin when she came to South Africa. I have come to love this direct honest and very warm loving woman. Reading the reflections of her journey, and having seen the openness in her heart personally, I can feel the power behind her clear messages of how to live authentically.

Everything works in divine intervention, so it was synchronistic when Robin asked me to read her book because I was experiencing an existential crisis of my own. I was in the space of questioning my connectedness to the God source, ironic isn't it? I was about to publish my first book, getting married in two weeks and ready to launch a brand new project doing what I loved, but yet I missed seeing God in all this busyness. I had a need to sense God like I did before in the silence. How many clients have I coached on the very topic of 'How do I connect with God?' That is when the "ETA2 Oneness" message echoed in my being:

*"WHEN WE THINK WE KNOW, WE DON'T.
WE ARE ASSUMING AND NOT LISTENING
TO GOD."*

When we ask again and again: 'where is God?', Robin reminded me that 'He/She' has gone nowhere, but it is I whom experience myself as a "separate self" because I experience myself as thoughts and emotions from a separate identity. To feel the connection (which is always there) I need to ASK and know that I DON'T KNOW. Answers only come from God when my mind stops pretending to know what the answers already are.

This book is for you if you achieved it all, and also if you are seeking but cannot find. If you are in the place where you need to refine your values and are ready to enter a new wave of consciousness that is hitting this planet, you will love the profound truths that are recorded here.

To stay in an authentic "open heart space" is not an achievement. It is a moment to moment willingness to feel your inner guidance and see God's hand in your daily life. The billboards and children's smiles communicate God source to us if we are prepared to notice it. Everything is a reflection of us and the work to be done to connect to God source is inside of us. What you will get here is just how to do that.

Thank you Robin for sharing what is in your heart. When we reach from the highest part within ourselves, we are bound to self-regulate our beliefs. Time to unlearn and remap what we think we know, not because it is written in a book but because it resonates deeply within our soul. A woman is truly powerful when her vulnerability is beautiful. Authenticity heals, but first we need to feel.

Adele Green
Author and Life Coach
South Africa

Preface

Since becoming an adult, I spent time pondering some of life's difficult questions. Is it possible to practice my spiritual principles of tolerance, patience, kindness and love in a world full of violence, hatred, aggression and selfishness? Is it possible to really be in "oneness" with God if I follow the blueprint left by Jesus as written in the Bible? Is it possible to trust "divine guidance" when I don't trust anybody or anything? Is it possible to reconcile my spiritual philosophy with my human behavior? I took on the study of these questions as a hobby for 20 years while working as a management consultant.

I immersed myself in analysis while reading sacred texts from the world's major religious traditions including: Christianity, Judaism, Islam, Taoism, Hinduism and Buddhism. I integrated my study of religion with travel to 40 countries around the world where these religious traditions are practiced including: Italy, Israel, Egypt, China, India, Thailand and Peru. It doesn't take any effort to intellectually ponder these questions, but it takes a lot of courage to pursue the answers.

After manifesting the "American Dream" of money and privilege, billing my client $70,000 per month, I was shocked to find I felt separated and isolated from God. The longer I pursued the "American Dream" the more dissatisfied I became until one day I remembered seeing Debbie Ford, New York Times Bestselling Author on Oprah talking about her concepts. Bingo!!!

I instantly realized what was missing from my life was access to my own emotionality which had been tied up with past trauma. Afraid to fully express for fear of what would emerge, I hunkered down in trying to reach God through the intellectual concepts in my mind. As Debbie Ford was fond of saying, the "longest journey is the one from your head to your heart."

I pursued a certified life coaching certificate taking classes under Debbie Ford as a way to access more of my buried emotionality and to uncover my "shadow beliefs" which kept me repeating the same old patterns in my life. Over time, as I learned to own my "contribution to the chaos", I was able to forgive myself and others totally releasing us all. The past was no longer the arbiter of my future.

With access to my emotionality, I was now ready to continue my spiritual journey and reunite my soul with the "Source of all creation". So you can imagine my shock when

I found out I would have to risk the loss of everything I had manifested in order to access "oneness" with God. Hoping others can benefit from my story, I have detailed my wild and crazy journey to spiritual awakening and the resulting process which has come to be known as the estimated time of arrival to oneness (ETA 2 Oneness).

Acknowledgement

You have often heard it said, "It takes a village to raise a child". Well, I would modify that statement to say, "It takes a village to anchor any new idea".

With that in mind, I would like to thank my friend and life coach Adele Green from South Africa for reading the manuscript and agreeing to write the forward. It was touching to know the words in this book were helpful to someone who lives half-way around the world.

I would like to also thank Danielle Bonnefil-Wahab, my tri-lingual editor and friend of 25 years for her continued support of the concepts in this book aimed at moving the world towards "oneness".

All new ideas stay in the realm of unreality until you allow others to read and offer feedback as to the validity of the ideas. Many thanks to Deborah Heist, Madrid Jacobs-Brown, Dr. C Vanessa White and Linda Brown for taking time to read a draft of this book. Your validation of many of the concepts in the book was much appreciated.

Special thanks to Aurelia Saunders-Satchell for going that extra mile as my proofreader making all of the necessary corrections so the reader did not get sidetracked by focusing on the mistakes and miss the central message of the book.

There are those in life who continue to give you encouragement because they have traveled similar spiritual paths. To my life coaching buddies Sharon Jackson, Rochelle Schwartz, Kristina Hess, and Alisha Schwartz, I thank you from the bottom of my heart for sharing your stories and encouraging me to continue anchoring spiritual life coaching concepts in my own life.

Much is made of the role of family support, I am blessed to have very supportive family members backing me up and testing out some of these concepts in their own lives. Grateful I am for the love and support of my mother, Shirley M. Dennis and my sisters, Pamela Johnson and Sherrie Grasty.

In order to have a strong spiritual foundation, it is necessary to spend time in a community of believers. Thanks for the support provided me from Pastor Marshall Mitchell and the congregation of Salem Baptist Church of Jenkintown located in suburban Philadelphia, PA. *To God be the glory for the things he has done.*

Introduction

What happens to my life if I don't guide it? Will my life fall apart because I do not set daily intentions, create action steps, or repeat daily affirmations? Is there really a God that will step in and take control if I completely let go? Or will my life descend into such chaos that it is impossible to repair the damage that I have created? Is there something I am doing which is blocking me from oneness with God and limiting my ability to share love and kindness with all that is? These were the questions that I asked myself in the spring of 2009. I felt ready to take the journey to spiritual awakening because I felt pulled by something greater than myself. I felt pulled by a deep seated urge to be in the true oneness with God, the divine source of my creation.

It is funny how we can be on "top of the world" and choose that moment to make the kind of decision that can impact our lives forever. When I decided to pursue oneness and connectivity to God above all else, I had no idea what was about to happen to my life. I was living a wonderful life having achieved the "American Dream" with access to all of the money that I desired since I was the prime contractor on a $2 million contract. My monthly invoice billed to a consulting client was approximately $70,000 per month with a substantial amount of that going into my pocket. Surely, it was not money issues that were motivating me to make the change.

When you have money, it is true that you can do a lot of things on your "bucket list" which can bring you happiness. For me, my deepest desire involved traveling the world. I was now able to travel to any country that I longed to see so that is exactly what I did. I visited sacred sites such as Machu Picchu in Peru, Great Wall in China, Pyramids in Egypt, Western Wall in Israel, Robben Island in South Africa, Taj Mahal in India, Summer Palace in Russia and even the Opera House in Australia. If a place called to me, like magic I could be there in a flash. This rash of international travel slowed as I approached 40 countries that I had visited around the world. Don't get me wrong, there are still a few places left on my "bucket list" but the burning desire to travel no longer pulls me like it once did.

With access to money, there are a lot of tangible and material things you can purchase for your own amusement. During my international travels, I shopped for clothing and jewelry. When I got home, I had my symbols of success including my BMW sports coupe and my 24 speed BMW bicycle both parked outside side my typically suburban house. In addition, I was fortunate that my house was only one block from the local mall with stores like Macy's, Bloomingdales, Nordstrom's, Coach and my favorite restaurant the Cheesecake Factory. What could be better!

You may be thinking that I was living a charmed life but up to this point in the story I was missing one important component as a single woman…I felt I needed a "man" to make me complete. Yes, as a typical woman, despite my claims of independence, I still desired to have a relationship in my life to validate my very existence. I had bought into the hype that "you are nothing without a man". So I opened up my heart while doing all of the things I could to manifest the man of my dreams. In no short time, he appeared. He was made to order with his model good looks, tall, dark, handsome with brains to match since he was Ivy League educated. Ah, but is he spiritual you may ask? The answer to that was "yes" as we spent long hours in discussion about God and spiritual awakening. My life could not have been better at the time I decided to step away from it all.

What would make me do such a thing? What would make me leave this "ideal life" that most people are trying so hard to achieve? What would make me think there was something more valuable than what I was already experiencing? To my surprise, the basic answer was that all of what I was engaged in seemed to take an unusual amount of energy pulling me off of my center with God instead of anchoring me. Therefore, the more I tried to hold onto the dream that I had manifested for myself, based on society standards, the more disconnected and unhappy I became.

Everywhere I turned in my life, I seemed to be confronted with disagreements to manage, entitlements to control and frustrations to diffuse. I often began to ask myself, "Where is God in all of this 'ego madness' while I was playing master of my universe"? I began to feel the sadness I was experiencing was because I was no longer living with God at the center of my world. Because I had lived the "American dream", I could now say for certain it was not the road to "oneness" that I had imagined it would be. Having achieved all I desired, the pull of my human self was starting to give way to the pull of my divine self.

Looking For Love in All the Wrong Places

It was time to make the big decision and get an answer to my question, "What happens to my life if I don't guide it? I had summoned up the courage to find out. One by one I started to make changes in my life. The first change I made was to break off my relationship. As it sometimes happens in relationships, there can be conflict when there are differences in values. In this case, there were major differences in how to connect to God. In my being, I knew access to God was not in the rituals so I constantly resisted instruction from my friend on how to meditate and pray in order to reach God. From my personal experience, I could speak to God at any time either laying down or sitting up because I had a personal relationship with God. So the more I tried to accommodate my mate using rituals, the less connected I felt to the "God of my understanding".

How could this relationship which held so much promise be full of such conflict? With time and distance, I could begin to see that I created an image in my mind and manifested it with my strong desires but never once gave thought to my partner's needs. In my mind, he was created to totally satisfy me, my desires, my wishes, and my fantasy. The problem was that his behavior was reflecting back to me my own selfishness and limited way of thinking. It was then that I had my own "ah ha" moment. I realized that anything which originates in the mind is created by the ego which is only about the "I" not about the "we".

As a result of this realization, I learned there was no way to create a desire in my mind, then focus my attention on manifesting it with the expectation that others will equally enjoy what I created for my own benefit. No wonder I was having so much conflict in my relationship. Am I alone in experiencing this kind of thinking? Have you ever tried to create an ideal relationship in your mind but not have the willingness to deal with the needs of the person who showed up? Not accounting for this reality allowed my beautiful vision to turn into a terrible nightmare. Before the nightmare was over, I had the opportunity to take a good hard look at my own belief system. What void within myself was I trying to fill? So many questions but so few answers...

As the months of separation rolled on, I continued to maul over the questions confronting me. How come I was so willing to abandon myself and lose myself in this relationship? What finally brought the relationship to an end was this feeling that I was somehow being separated from the "essential essence" of who I was. I decided that no relationship was worth separating me from God. I could no longer absorb society's belief that compromising myself for a man would somehow make me happy.

It was primarily against this belief system that I rebelled. I allowed my true feelings of frustration, unhappiness, anxiety and even depression to surface sealing in the belief that no relationship is worth holding on to that makes me feel unloved simply because it gave me the proper persona. It seems like sometimes we are looking for love in all the wrong places when the love that is truly needed comes from our connection to God.

It's unfortunate that when we break up relationships there is anger and hostility that lingers. This was no exception. Several months passed with no communication before I decided to open the channels. I believed that in order to heal, we both needed to give each other permission to fully express and vent the anger and hostility that was in our hearts. True to this new generation of communicators, we held our most intimate of conversations over the internet.

We sent scathing email messages back and forth to each other until we both felt free that we had said all we needed to say.

As peace descended between us, my heart again felt peace as I knew separating from him had been the right thing for me. Many of us hold onto relationships that do not quite fit because we find it more acceptable to be in a relationship than to be without one. I had decided my happiness was important to me not just from a selfish point of view but because when I am feeling happy, I seem to have better access to the spirit of God within.

Money and Misplaced Values

The second thing I needed to do in order to take my "ego world" apart was to step away from a career I had created including the high paying contracts. This was going to be the ultimate challenge. In the spring of 2009 I was coming to the end of a fantastic consulting contract in which I was invoicing my client almost $70,000 per month. I had the option of continuing the contract but I decided against it. The main reason for my decision was because I found where there is a lot of money, everyone seems to hold the thought that more of the money should go to them. This produces conflict because the same dollars cannot go to different people. I found many of the individuals working for me were always looking for ways to justify taking more of the money for themselves. With everyone knowing the budget but not the expenses, it seemed to foster a sense of entitlement that came with the contract process.

At this time in my life, I had just turned 50 years old and was getting very tired of managing people's egos. Now add to that the burden of feelings of entitlement being displayed by people who I had known for years. It became a toxic soup. Somehow, somewhere we have all absorbed the belief "money equals security". Therefore, the more you have, the better off you are. We have lost sight of our spiritual roots in this materialistic society and I was no exception to that rule. From my spiritual studies, money is the external manifestation of internal divine guidance. It is this divine guidance which is responsible for the creation of something that brings the money. For money in and of itself is not the thing to be pursued nor controlled instead access to God for divine guidance is what should be desired.

Trying to stop people from the "land grab" that had become this contract was indeed an unwanted professional nightmare that was running concurrent with my personal relationship nightmare. There must be a "new way of being" that is not so contentious with others. How could I lessen the constant conflict that comes when there is a lot of money involved? I no longer had the ability to endure such conflict and chaos just for the sake of making money. It was taking too much out of me emotionally. More importantly, once again I was beginning to feel a separation from the spirit of

God within me. The more I turned my attention to trying to control the money grabbing people all around me, the more I felt angry, frustrated, depressed and hopeless as they often threatened to "stop work" or "sue me" if there was dissatisfaction with contract assignments.

This professional situation, like my personal situation was something I was "not" prepared to be entangled in over a long period of time. When I finally made the decision to let go of the contract, "I felt very relieved" and thanked God it was over. I then laughed to myself and said "you must be completely crazy, do you know how many people would want to be in your position billing a client at a rate of $70,000 per month"! I was living a dream that some people couldn't even begin to conceptualize. It wasn't long before I crash landed when my ego raged out of control with concerns such as: What could be more important than having access to that kind of money? How will you ever replace that kind of income? How will you survive? What are you really looking for in life does not exist? What is wrong with you? There were so many questions at this time in my life that I declined to ponder.

Time of Restoration

After achieving a level of success, I had reached a point where I felt there must be more to life than the pursuit of money, relationships, and other individual goals. I began to believe that life was more than just satisfying my own ego desires. Sure, I set goals and achieved them. I set intentions and experienced them. I repeated daily affirmations and bible scriptures. I had everything I wanted, but that did not bring me joy. All I felt was a temporary state of happiness until the next goal was set and achieved, like a junkie looking for his next "fix". This way of living did not produce permanent joy. All I wanted was a way out of the madness. So, I decided to set one last goal which was the "pursuit of oneness with God".

It was my hope that this new challenge to make God the center of my life would finally give me the *"peace that passes all understanding"*. I was looking forward to God *"ordering my steps"* and *"performing the tasks he had assigned for me to do"*. It was time to stop feeding my life force energy into my ego driven lifestyle. The questions continued. Is there more to life than the fulfillment of our personal agendas? Is there more to life than the fulfillment of society's standards? Where is God in the midst of all of this pursuit? The truth be known, as I stood on the "top of the world", there was such an emptiness inside of me despite the external accomplishments. What was missing in my life was my connection to my "essential essence". What was missing in my life was my connection to God. I was so busy "playing God" that only by pressing "pause" on my ego driven lifestyle could I clearly see my own ego (Easing God Out).

Once my life had officially slowed and I was no longer entangled, I felt awfully giddy and happy that I had made those decisions. I was clear I was not here to pursue my personal pleasures or to measure up to society standards. I was not here to be at the beck and call of everybody who needed me to fulfill their ego desires. I was here for a different purpose and now I was about to find out what that was. For in my heart, I always believed my divine destiny was tied up with a global movement to "oneness". The fact that my life was so far out of control and so distant from the concept of peace and harmony, I knew beyond a shadow of a doubt that I was on the wrong track despite the accolades given to me for my accomplishments. I soon learned to ask, "Just because something is applauded by others, is it also something automatically applauded by you"?

As I reflect back on my life in the spring of 2009, I could see a time when I could do what I wanted, go where I wanted, or buy what I wanted. Every day, all day long, my life was my own with no boss, no boyfriend, and no demands on my time. Oh what freedom I experienced. Life was truly a new adventure. I cannot begin to tell you the peace that came over me the more distant I got from the world that I had created. I woke up every morning with a smile on my face and met each morning with a simple phrase, "Good Morning God". I started my mornings doing daily prayer (me talking to God) and meditation (me listening to God). In my moments of prayer, I was thanking

God for getting me out of the situations that were causing me so much unhappiness. In my meditation time, I was open with a listening ear to being used by God for what it was that God wanted to share with me.

As the spring turned to summer my connection to my spirit grew stronger. I could feel God's presence all around me especially as I spent more time outdoors. There was nothing better than communing with God in nature with the flowers in bloom, birds chirping in the background and the sun on my face. I also took advantage of the warm weather to put my body back into balance as I found myself riding my bike an average of four miles per day or enjoying a walk through the woods and around the lake. My diet consisted of cooking tons of veggies on the grill. When I think back on that summer, I can only smile.

As my summer gave way to fall, the green leaves gave way to red, orange and yellow as the beauty of fall was in full splendor. I could not believe I had been given the last six months for such a period of restoration for my weary soul. Life could not have been better. For sure, I started to believe *"when the praises go up, the blessings do come down"*. Now that I felt rested and relaxed from my summer fun, I started reading more of my spiritual books including the Bible because I knew that my destiny was tied up in a new understanding of my divine purpose.

Signs of My Divine Destiny

During the early part of the fall I received a call from one of my cousins who asked me to go with her to Australia to a conference of world religions. At this point in my life, I had been to all of the major continents but Australia, and had nothing on the schedule, so I decided to go. Attending this conference seemed to be the right occasion since I would be interacting with people who practiced all of the religions that I had studied including: Christianity, Judaism, Islam, Buddhism, Hinduism and Taoism. There were to be 8,000 representatives from all parts of the world coming together in peace and harmony to share information on making religion more useful and applicable in bringing the world together in oneness.

Coming back from that conference, I felt my mission, my divine destiny, my purpose were becoming clearer. I was never more excited or "on fire" to join in the movement of the world towards oneness. The world religion conference showed how truly interconnected we all are and how with God at the center of our being, no one seemed to be a stranger. I have never been at such a large conference where everyone was just as eager to talk to you as you were to talk to them about our individual ways of honoring God. What could be more important than living in oneness with God, self and others?

Now I knew beyond a shadow of a doubt why I walked away from the life that I was living. The life that I had created did not have at its core the recognition of God, therefore the decisions that I'd made in my life were ego based without the needs of others in mind. Sadly, this is the way much of the Western world is operating. I wondered if this "great spiritual awakening" would be able to penetrate through our veil of self- absorption so we could see our connectivity to "all that is".

"What is this spiritual awakening"? In order to find out the answer, I had to get still and allow the silence of my mind to bring forward the answer. To my surprise the answer that I was given, was fairly simple. The voice of my spirit said, "The great spiritual awakening is simply allowing the presence of God to sit at the center of our being and guide all of our decisions from a place of love". So my next question was, "how do I know when God is sitting at the center of my being"? The answer that came back was, "God is at the center of your being when the results of your decisions produce joy for not only yourself but for others as well".

As my conversation with God continued, I got clarity on the concept of how to attain "joy". I was told that sometimes people misunderstand that joy is the "result of being in spiritual alignment with God" and "not a goal to be pursued". What? How can that be? I have been told all of my life to "pursue my passion", "follow my bliss", and "do what makes me happy" in order to live in joy. Now I am being told that these ways of being will not bring me joy if I am not in spiritual alignment. What other spiritual beliefs would have to be modified or nullified on the road to oneness?

Preparing the Vessel for Spiritual Alignment

In my study and communion time with God, it was becoming increasingly clear that I needed to prepare my vessel for spiritual alignment. What is my part in this spiritual alignment process? Answer, I need to "clean out the vessel". What is the vessel? I am the vessel. What needs to be cleaned out? My heart needs clearing of all memories that contain pain, negativity, judgment, hopelessness, anger, victimization and the resulting behaviors that go with these emotions. That is a lot to ask a person to release the traumatic memories that have created our way of operating in reality. But, that is exactly what needs to happen in order to bring oneself into spiritual alignment with God.

The spiritual alignment we are all seeking is not merely the reciting of bible verses or affirmations but the ability to "live God's word". The Bible is not simply a book to be read, but a roadmap for transformation. Anchoring this new way of being will require we shift our values to allow our belief system to put God in control of our lives. What makes this different from how humans currently function is that we say God is in control, but then proceed to make all of our own decisions. Once we have outlined where and how our lives should be, we then contact God through prayer and submit our list of requests we want God to fulfill. This way of thinking can no longer be. Central to this new thought system is that our skills and talents are for God's use in building God's kingdom here on earth. Our only role is one of "spiritual obedience" to the will of God since we cannot see totality as God does, we cannot speak with any certainty on how God can best use us.

I have studied many methodologies that will allow us to clean out the vessel, all of which say it is important to have as your foundation a "spiritual understanding of who and what God is to you". Those who attend church or other religious institutions have an advantage in building this foundation because their study of sacred texts gives them the philosophical underpinnings. Those who have faced a major personal crisis such as cancer, divorce, bankruptcy, death of a loved one or loss of job are more likely to know God on an intimate basis. In order to know God aright, you must find yourself in a place of human weakness to experience first-hand God's strength.

False Start

After the conference in Australia I really believed I knew what had to be done to bring myself into spiritual alignment with God. I had been working on cleaning out my vessel for more than 20 years. I believed God was with me in guiding my hand in the writing of my first book entitled, "Awakening of a Chocolate Mystic". In this book, I start off talking about "mastering our appetites" for the pleasures and addictions of this world. For it is only by the mastering of our appetites for things like food, alcohol, drugs, sex, money and even love that we are able to shift ourselves to a higher spiritual frequency.

After this book was written I really believed it was my destiny to share this type of information. However, I soon found out that it did not take my ego long to try and take over this new spiritual process. During my prayer time, I found myself telling God what would and would "not" work in trying to distribute my first book. It is really easy to get caught up when you think you know the way. Think twice, for if you think you know the way, you can be assured you have now lost your way because your "spiritualized ego" has hijacked the process. To move into spiritual alignment with God allowing for the oneness with others requires moving in a direction that you do not understand. That direction can only come from the spirit of God that is deep within you that is tailored to your particular understanding.

As you think you are ready to share your thoughts with the world, you must first understand where your information is coming from that you are bringing forward. I had studied the concepts of spiritual awakening for decades. I was part of a community of believers and attended church regularly. I just knew I had the foundation that God needed to use me to speak truth. However what I did not understand was that God gives information on a "need to know only basis" focusing attention always in the now.

What I found myself doing was projecting out three months, six months or even one year in terms of what needed to happen to launch myself as an author and speaker on spiritual matters. As I continued to take my spiritual understanding and put it to work in a very human way to create what I thought God wanted… things began to fall apart. The book sales that were rising initially began to plummet in direct proportion to the amount of control I tried to exercise over the process. Finally, I had to press "pause" again on my life and get reconnected.

I found out how easily we can take spiritual concepts and filter them through our egos allowing our ego to hijack the process for its own personal agenda. I did it very easily without even the slightest clue as to what was happening. Even after studying all of the philosophical concepts and spending hours in communion with God, I was quickly lost on my journey to spiritual awakening. In so many ways, I felt like I was back at "square one". Doubt had now seeped in as I wondered if spiritual alignment was really even possible for human beings.

With my doubt and resulting feelings of separation from God came the ego-based questioning, "Did I do the right thing by stepping away from my job, my career, and my relationship"? I thought I knew the way to God. I thought that I understood what God needed from me. Now I was totally unsure. But, how could this be? As I uploaded my theology, I remembered *"all things work together for good for those who love God"*. However in my life at the moment everything was not working together for good, things were falling apart. I soon learned that our lives will "not" always be the way we think they will be when we follow divine guidance, because *"God's ways are not our ways"*.

How Did I Get This So Wrong

Where do I go from here? I am too far in to turn around. It has been more than two years since my last contract and I am no closer to understanding what it is that God wants me to do. How did I get this so wrong? The enthusiasm from the conference in Australia was far in my rearview mirror, but I felt myself being pulled forward by my determination to bring forth a "new way of being" which was still very much anchored in my heart. I knew God had a divine destiny for me as God has a destiny for everyone. However it is really hard to move in that direction when each step forward seems to be met with two steps backwards?

As the days turned into months and now the months have turned into years, I felt no closer to what I was supposed to do for God. My life was spiraling out of control. Anxiety started to become the order of the day as my financial situation was taking a nose dive. How am I supposed to stay calm and focus my attention on God during my meditations when the phone is ringing off the hook with creditors looking for payments? What is happening to my life? I thought I knew what my spiritual assignment was on God's behalf. How did I get the message so wrong? Where do I go from here?

As I stilled my anxious heart, I soon realized I needed to go back to God and totally surrender the idea of being a spiritual author and speaker even though I felt it was my destiny. The surrender took the form of stillness and silence as I stopped trying to take action steps. This total lack of momentum was soon followed by sadness, depression and lots of tears. Have I wasted the last two years of my life? Is it really possible to find God in this dimension of reality? Is God only supposed to be an intellectual concept? I have failed to do what I always believed in my heart was possible. I have failed to become one with the spirit of God within me.

After my daily emotional reactions to what was "not" happening in my world, I finally began to feel a little calmer with the passing of time. My surrender was beginning to grow as I stopped trying to push forward what I thought ought to be happening. I also stopped responding to the credit collection agencies. At last, I remember sleeping very soundly one night with no idea what I dreamt about but upon awakening I felt energized. There was a sense of peace and joy that I seemed to find in my soul although there was no reason for it.

As was my ritual, I did a quick morning prayer before getting out of bed then proceeded to go and take a shower. While in the shower I felt so good that I just began singing the chorus from one of my favorite church hymns… "*I don't believe he brought me this far… I don't believe he brought me this far… to leave me*". All of a sudden I heard this very clear voice which I knew to be the spirit of God within give new information. I had not heard my spirit speaking in months so I was both surprised and delighted to be reconnected in such a powerful way.

ETA 2 Oneness

The message I got in the shower was as follows. You will teach a program called "ETA 2 Oneness". This phrase is written as a text language that really means "estimated time of arrival to oneness"? Oh I like that, I remembered thinking to myself. The question to be answered by everyone is, "What is your estimated time of arrival to oneness with God, self and others? The message continued as there is a double meaning for the phrase "ETA 2 Oneness". Each letter will represent part of the process for teaching people how to move into oneness. The letter "E" means "Embrace your authentic emotionality". The letter "T" means "Trust divine guidance". Finally the letter "A" means "Anchor a new way of being".

Using spiritual life coaching techniques, you will support others in reconciling their spiritual beliefs with their human behaviors thereby opening their hearts to becoming "clear channels of pure love". From this place, individuals will be guided in the use of their unique talents and abilities in the building of the kingdom of God. You will "not" be known as the founder of "ETA 2 Oneness" instead you will be known as a "facilitator" because this information has been given to you, "not" created by you. Oh snap, did that really just happen?

When I least expected it, I was released from this holding space in which I felt disconnected from God. I was so happy to realize that I really do have a divine destiny to support others on their spiritual journey. I always felt I had something special I was supposed to do here on earth and now that information had come to me. Where do we begin?

I went to church with an open heart the following Sunday because I now felt I was getting divine guidance. While in church I read the newsletter which advertised for teachers for our church Bible Institute. In the moment after I finished reading this, I heard the voice of my spirit tell me, "You shall teach here". I remembered thinking I must be getting this wrong. I have always been a "bench member" in church never belonging to any organization. However, you could count on me to always attended major functions such as banquets or special services.

Since hearing the message in the shower, this was the first time I was truly being asked to be "spiritually obedient". I had a little trouble letting go of my analytical mind. Since the message was completely out of "left field" telling me to teach in church, I started second guessing myself about whether I heard the message correctly. When I got home from church, I walked around in circles in my living room, taking time to glance out of the big picture window as I asked God: "Am I really supposed to teach spiritual life coaching techniques in a Baptist church"? This has never been done before. Will they be open to such concepts? The only way to find out was to make contact with the Dean of the Bible Institute and share with her my experience.

The next day was Monday and despite my nervousness I made a telephone call to the Dean. To my surprise, she listened closely to what I had to say, then told me that if God was leading me in this direction, that I needed to follow through. She invited me to attend the meeting of the teachers of the Bible Institute which was scheduled for the following day. When I hung up the phone I just stared at the phone in utter amazement. When God tells you to do something, your only job is to "answer the call". Needless to say the meeting went well with the other teachers and before I knew it I was teaching spiritual life coaching seminars at my church. The sessions were well attended.

The new challenge I started to experience was the creation of the curriculum to be taught. I had learned from my past experience to wait on God and not run ahead thinking I knew the way. So each week before every seminar, I waited on my spirit to give me information which always seemed to come at the last minute as if my spirit was waiting for something. In the end, it always turned out to be exactly what that particular audience needed to hear. It is from this place I began to understand that when God is working through you it is no longer up to you to decide what needs to be shared or what actions need to be taken. I began to relax and know for sure that my destiny was no longer of my making.

Is Your Life Collapsing?

Many of us at this time in our lives are experiencing great difficulties. Have you lost your house to foreclosure? Have you lost your job to downsizing? Have you lost your business to a bad economy? Have you lost your car to repossession? Have you lost a relationship to separation or divorce? Have you lost your health to accident or illness? I don't know how many of these things are true for you, but for me I am having many of these experiences all at once. It's as if my whole life is collapsing but I am not sure yet what is replacing it. It is only my trust in God that is allowing me to move through these experiences and accept that I am "losing things that no longer serve me."

We sometimes believe that experiences are coming to us because we have somehow failed to "learn the lessons". This may be why such great emphasis is placed on looking back and reviewing our life's experiences. Are you tired of looking back in order to look ahead? Would you believe me, if I told you that looking back serves no purpose? Aren't we supposed to get the lessons, you might ask? Isn't that how we avoid repeating mistakes?

As humans, we are greatly misguided in our understanding about "mistakes". To us, a mistake is an "unwanted outcome". In our ego mind, we somehow believe that we know what is "best" for us. Would you believe me, if I told you there was no such thing as a mistake? For everything that happens to you, is what is supposed to happen to you for your own spiritual growth and development. To me, many difficult experiences stem from not living in the oneness with God where decisions are God-centered. For how can you consider any outcome to be a mistake if you are following the guidance of God? From this place, there are no mistakes nor are there any lessons to be learned, for everything is in divine order.

When Good is Not Good Enough

How do we get into this oneness with God? I thought I knew from my spiritual study and world travels what it meant to be a "good person" and a "good Christian". I thought being a "good person" was all I needed to do to be in the oneness with God and others. So you can imagine my shock and dismay at finding out that I was neither a "good person" nor a "good Christian" by a new set of values uncovered in my spiritual life coaching process. I found out I did not have an objective way to measure my "goodness" because of how society had shaped my belief system. I unconsciously looked for the "accolades" in my "altruism" never understanding my true intentions and motivations.

As my mother once said, "the key to being a 'good person' means you do for people knowing in advance that they may 'not be grateful' or even say 'thank you' for the things you have done". One of the giant steps for Christians is to be able to do "good" no matter how people respond. Are you seeing yourself as philosophically "good" with the corresponding deeds lagging far behind? As Jesus is reported to have said, *"None is good but the father"*. In your definition of "goodness", do you include the consideration of the needs of your brothers and sisters as equal to your own? Remember, there is no "single admission ticket" available to "oneness"…

Sleepwalking Through Life

As I tried to live in the oneness with God, I came to realize I was really "sleepwalking" through life. How do you know if you are sleepwalking through life? Simple, if you create conflict or chaos in your decision making process then your guide in life is your ego and not the spirit of God. How do you wake up, you might ask? The answer is "not" so simple and often unacceptable. I found that in order to wake up from sleepwalking through life, I had to be ready for "my world to collapse" as I found my ego under the rubble.

We are so invested in our own intelligence; we are so "puffed up" that we could "not" possibly know the way to God. It is the arrogance of our ego that insists we do know the way. Despite my intellectual understanding of God, I was never able to truly "feel" the presence of God. Fortunately for me as I continued my pursuit of God, taking risk far beyond my capacity to handle, my ego let go and God stepped in. It took me 20 years of prayer, study, and globetrotting to understand that God is more than an intellectual concept. God can be felt in our everyday experiences. The presence of God is nearly invisible if we determine the purpose of our experiences is to wrap ourselves up in selfish desires and pursuits. I learned through trial and error that I am "not" here for me, I am here for God. It is not for God to join my will, but for me to join with God's will. I had it twisted!

For me, my destiny has everything to do with my willingness to be spiritually obedient. It is my spiritual assignment as the facilitator of "ETA 2 Oneness" to bring forward new information that God is sharing through me. You have learned a lot about my story and my spiritual philosophy up to this point, now I am excited to share with you more of the details. I am hopeful this will inspire you on your own journey to spiritual awakening. Are you ready and willing to see your own life's experiences in a new light?

PART I

Embrace Your Authentic Emotionality

CHAPTER 1

Confronting Painful Memories

When it comes to painful memories, isn't it better to let "sleeping dogs lie"? You can if you want, but the cost will be continued isolation and/or conflict in your life. One of the biggest obstacles to becoming a "clear channel for God's use" is the carrying of emotional baggage which distorts our way of seeing reality. This can cause us to attack when no such attack is warranted.

In spiritual life coaching, this way of being is part of a concept called "projection" in which you criticize behavior in others when you cannot own or acknowledge the trait or behavior within yourself. In addition, you often displace your negative emotions of anger or hostility onto someone else. Unfortunately, we live in a world where we are all "projecting" all over each other! No wonder so many of our relationships are in chaos.

We all have a vital role to play in interrupting this pattern in our own lives. Would you like instead to experience the "oneness" which comes from living in peace and harmony with others? To this, most of us would say "yes". The disagreement comes in "how" to achieve this level of oneness.

God created each of us unique. Somehow we have come to believe that our individual view of reality is the correct one not just for ourselves but for others as well. To go one step further, many of us believe that if more people would just be like "us" the world would be a better place! For a long time, I too held this point of view. It never dawned on me that this arrogant way of thinking which allows for only "one right way" is synonymous with "ego"…"easing God out".

Many of our daily decisions are made with our egos which have not released emotional baggage, so those decisions are being made from a closed heart. The result will not permit solutions to be optimal or inclusive. Much of our conflict and chaos in our personal or professional lives comes from decisions made by others which are ego-based. We can never achieve oneness from this kind of thinking.

We can open our hearts by releasing our emotional baggage. As we increase our capacity to be clear channels for God's use, we can effortlessly share pure love with everyone and everything. In order to achieve this, it is time to "*put away childish things*" which are often the creations of our selfish egos.

Make no mistake I believe our egos have served a good purpose often protecting us from hurt, harm or danger when we were in situations in which we felt powerless. Much of the pain of our past has now crystallized into behavior that our ego uses to interact with the world today. We have grown up but our ego has not kept pace leaving us feeling limited or constrained in our emotional reactions. It is time for us to transcend our ego into the oneness of God.

All of us have had trauma in our lives which shaped our personalities. Most of us never took the time to sort out or resolve those painful memories that created who we thought we were. All of us are "walking wounded" as we have been victims of man's inhumanity to man. Some of us have seen the worst that man has to offer being first-hand victims of sexual abuse, physical abuse, or verbal abuse. So, how do we get beyond being the "walking wounded"? How do we begin to dismantle our ego? How do we begin to see the "true essence" of who God made us to be beyond our personalities? That is the subject of embracing your authentic emotionality.

Limiting or Shadow Beliefs

One of the biggest stumbling blocks on the road to oneness with God is the unwillingness of humans to see their "limiting" or "shadow" beliefs. My mentor and New York Best-Selling author Debbie Ford once said a shadow belief is "anything we hide, deny, suppressed, or repress because we view it as bad or wrong". For those on the spiritual path, if you tend to deny any aspect of yourself, you allow yourself to stay anchored to your ego. We must begin to address those limiting or shadow beliefs in ourselves that we hide within our innocence.

Many of us move through life feeling victimized at the hands of others but rarely do we look at what we have done to "contribute to the chaos". No doubt, others are wrong in their treatment of us but sometimes it is just much easier to project our negative feelings and emotions onto them rather than to look deeply within to focus on our own "bad behavior". Until we connect ourselves to our own projections and take full responsible for our contribution to the chaos, we will continue to experience conflict and chaos in our lives resulting in separation from others.

There is no way to contain a shadow belief indefinitely for it will show up at the worst possible time. It may be the display of "rage" when a situation calls for "calm". Do not cover it, but acknowledge the darkness within that the shadow belief seeks to hide. This may require some "good Christians" to put on pause the spiritual beliefs that do not allow you to be authentic in your emotionality long enough to integrate these shadow beliefs into the totality of your self-perception. It is only by taking this approach that you free yourself from the "separate self" you have created allowing your "divine self" to emerge. For who you have created yourself to be is not who you truly are.

An important spiritual concept that many of us would benefit greatly from understanding is the "essential essence" of who God created you to be was never disturbed by the events of your life. This innermost part of you or the soul of your being is protected by God and therefore remains untouched by mankind even if your body might have suffered assault. This concept could help explain how Jesus could have said to his tormentors while dying on the cross, *"forgive them my father for they know not what they do."*

Your ego has created your self-image as a "vulnerable personality" based on assumptions and experiences about yourself. The main focus of the story most of us experience from our egos is one of lack and limitation which is reinforced in situations that leave us proclaiming… "I am unlovable"…"I am unworthy"… "I am not good enough"… or "I don't matter"… None of which is true in God's eyes. As we move through life with these unconscious beliefs in place, we tend to magnetize to ourselves situations and people to reinforce what we believe. If you ever have wondered why you have such losers as companions, then all you need do is look at your unconscious limiting beliefs.

In our religious communities, it is time to take a look at the shadow beliefs we employ to hide our humanness from God. While we say we know we are human, we do everything within our power to hide our faults and frailties. In this way we can appear to be in alignment with spiritual teachings. The problem we have is when it is most necessary for us to "live" our spiritual philosophy, we find ourselves falling short. When a situation calls for us to "turn the other cheek", our human reaction is to "knock somebody out". Sure, intellectually we know the proper spiritual philosophy but something stops us from demonstrating the love and compassion called for.

I would suggest the reason we cannot show love and compassion is because of our "alternative human belief system" which interprets actions making us feel as if we have been attacked. If we look closer, we will be able to see the darkness we are really hiding within then we could admit to ourselves that we are not as "pure" as the new fallen snow as we would like for others to believe. If we stop covering for our humanness, then we can begin to integrate the shadow beliefs.

We have to get beyond the pressure from our religious institutions to feel as if we already have it altogether. This need to cover our authentic emotional reactions, not our lack of understanding of the "Word" in the Bible or other spiritual texts, is what is perpetuating our shadow beliefs. Until we can be authentic in our emotionality releasing everything but the love for one another, then we will never be in the oneness with God. To be in the oneness with God requires us to be in oneness with one another.

How do you break the patterns of the shadow or limiting beliefs? The first thing you must do is to become aware of "what belief" are you trying to hide from the rest of the world. Are you hiding your own insecurities or limitations by denying you even have a problem? Are you projecting your criticism and judgment onto another so as to deflect any attention from yourself? Whatever your reason for not being honest and authentic in your emotional expression, you must become aware of it.

Next, you must realize that the limiting belief you hold is providing a "payoff" for you keeping certain behaviors in place. If you look deeply enough, you will often find a shadow belief was created around a painful experience. At that time, a certain way of behaving allowed you to cope with the situation. Unfortunately, life moves on and most often the situation you are protecting yourself from, "no longer exist in your current reality". It is time to let go of that old way of being.

Finally, to break a limiting belief pattern, you must look for the blessings in the experience you considered painful. As Debbie used to say, "There is gold in the dark". Some gift or talent has now emerged as a result of a painful experience. If you do not look for the blessings, you are only left with feelings of anger or hatred towards another. This helps to anchor your alternative belief system which goes against everything you have learned in your spiritual philosophy. Do not let any past experience separate you from the love you once shared with another.

CHAPTER 2

Feelings Are a Good Thing

Somehow we have come to believe the open display of emotions or the willingness to follow our true feelings is somehow "not" a good thing. As a result, many of us are hiding our feelings as we tend to "go along just to get along". However, God has given us the ability to feel and interact with the world around us, so let's see if we can arrive at a new concept with regards to the proper role of "feelings".

In this context, "emotional authenticity" really means to be connected to your true "feeling nature" which is more "intuitive" giving you information that you have no way of knowing or verifying before-hand. Negative emotional reactions are what happen to us when we hide our true feelings. From my spiritual study, the path to oneness with God is by way of your true feeling nature which allows your decisions to be optimal benefiting not only yourself but others as well.

Many of us hide our true feelings because we are "walking wounded" having been the recipients of bad behavior by others. As a result of this state of being emotionally wounded, too many of us have accepted the belief it is somehow selfish, wrong or inconsiderate to stand up for our truth and feel what we are feeling about a situation. We therefore compromise unnecessarily with others and allow their bad decisions to prevail.

Bottom line is that all of what we are doing in our humanness is engaging one ego with another ego. In that context there is no room for compromise. Somebody's ego will always dominate the situation resulting in one person always being unhappy in our "zero-sum" game. In order to move to a higher vibration, we must elevate ourselves to a place of priority within ourselves. The most important way is to recognize that you are important and that what you want and what you need is also important.

To stop the slide into "ego madness", you must always stand firm in what you believe is best for yourself. You cannot judge the behavior of others unless you first speak up about what it is that benefits you and see if they are willing to include your concerns in their decisions. Unless you express yourself, you will not avoid the trap of generating underlying resentment which contributes to your emotional baggage. It is time to stop the charade and be truthful with others. It serves no one to say that "everything is fine… when it's really not" or to do something that you "really don't want to do".

Every time you are inauthentic, there is a price to be paid within you. No one else will see the struggles that you are going through as you try to reconcile your true feelings with your external persona. Deep within your heart you know your true feelings about a situation. These true feelings are not something that will go away until they are fully expressed. Unfortunately, these emotions sometimes get expressed in a volcanic eruption over a little situation.

As we move into this new age of openness and oneness, there is a new level of emotional transparency that will be required. As we get beyond our separate ego self, many of us will begin to tune into the true feelings of another as hiding what is in your heart is no longer an option. You see, the new vibration requires *"everything that is hidden to come to the light"*.

Being True to Yourself

Remember, the reason to embrace your emotional authenticity is because it will allow for your spiritual alignment with God to increase your capacity to become a clear channel of pure love. The first step in this process is being true to "yourself". Do not get caught up in how somebody will react to you. Do not get caught up in what you think may happen as a result of holding your position. Do not get caught up in feeling that you will somehow be permanently isolated and separated from others because of your beliefs. Be willing to be alone in your decision for you run the risk of being alone anyway when your true feelings come to light.

There is no more hiding allowed in terms of our emotional decision-making. There is no more hiding behind inconsistent thought and actions…saying one thing and doing another. We must build a foundation of honesty within ourselves that brings forward consistency in word, thought and action. It is time to stand in your own truth… no exceptions… no excuses. From that place it becomes easier to deal with others.

I know this thought seems paradoxical and a little surprising because it seems to invite conflict. It really is easier because you are not standing on shifting sand but on the solid foundation of your principles and values. Your willingness to do this also allows others the same opportunity. This stops some of the push and pull we engage in to make people accommodate our ego desires. Also as you stand firm in your truth, it allows others to stand firm in their truth and from this place a genuine human compromise is achievable which begins to open the door to the divine.

Unfortunately, as humans we have to operate from this selfish place protecting our feelings and emotions until we resolve all of our own unexpressed emotionality. Once we have released our emotional baggage, we will be moving towards a place of oneness where our decisions will be inclusive as they affect not only ourselves but others. This is the ultimate in the decision-making process to have the ability to understand the impact of your decision on others. Right now the way we operate from our human self is to just make a decision and whatever the benefit is to us should be okay with everybody else. Guess what? It's not.

Walking Wounded

How do we get beyond being "walking wounded" to embrace our authentic emotionality? We must understand why we are walking wounded in the first place. The main reason we are walking wounded has to do with some behavior we experienced at the hands of our parents, guardians or caretakers. Sometimes I think we all forget that they too were influenced and affected by their parents, guardians and caretakers. Therefore we have generations of dysfunctional patterns passed down from one generation to the next.

Since most of us have had to deal with abuse or neglect in some form or fashion, we learned as children to protect ourselves from "abuse of authority" by creating different strategies which ultimately crystallized into our personalities. This is not a judgment on anyone's behavior but an explanation for a process that we seem to go through as humans.

I will use myself as an example. As a result of being a product of divorce by age three, I longed for unity and harmony from those around me. As a way to get this, I would often allow others to have their way no matter what the consequences were to me. This was being done for the sake of peace and harmony.

I would behave like this as long as I could until people's egos got "out of control". All of a sudden without my ability to control it, my repressed and unexpressed emotionality would just blow to the surface. Once calm, I would start the process all over again allowing people with stronger egos to dominate the situations. That way of being was not healthy for me and created a false persona of me as a "nice easy-going person" when in reality I was "not" that nice especially when you were not that considerate of my feelings.

Those of us who have been victims of abuse are truly the walking wounded. In too many instances, the walking wounded have turned into bullies, victimizers and intimidators themselves perpetuating this cycle of violence within humanity. One of the reasons why bullies get their way is because they become very aggressive and belligerent with others and use their anger as a "tool to force compliance".

Rather than confront them, most of us are not willing to go beyond the external façade of the bully to see what other rage lies within. So we cave to the demands of those we perceive as more powerful than ourselves. That may be beneficial for the bully, but it continues to create resentment and rage within far too many of us.

Each of us has been wounded because each of us has experienced pain or hurt by somebody over something. Unfortunately life moves on with new challenges to confront. Far too often, we never get a chance to fully express 100% of our pain. So, what happens to say the remaining 10% of this unexpressed emotion? I believe it simply gets buried. Over time, we continue to live life and have experiences where pain and hurt go unresolved. We compound this "residual emotionality" because we never allow ourselves time to truly heal opting instead for a strategy of "avoidance".

By being proactive to avoid situations that create pain, we believe we can avoid being hurt. This strategy without your awareness becomes part of the continuation of the negative pattern that you may be seeking to avoid. In some spiritual circles, this is called the "law of attraction" which operates whenever you put your attention on some desired outcome. Even if negative, it will manifest in your world. So be mindful of using the expression, "I don't want…" for that is exactly what you are going to get.

Since most of us tune in to past hurts, we keep our attention on negative patterns that might alert us to the fact that an "unwanted situation" is about to happen again. We become so vigilant in defending ourselves from potential harm; we actually begin creating the very situations we are seeking to avoid.

Let's look further into this concept. As already said, we are so busy trying to avoid the situation that has brought us harm in the past, we are on the lookout for anything which might remind us of that situation. As a result any small thing that happens may trigger us to perceive an external threat where none truly exist.

It is our interpretation of events causing us to react when that may not be the intention of the perceived offending party. It is our meaning we assign to somebody else's behavior that is creating the conflict we continue to experience, not the person's actual behavior. We are the ones responsible for our own beliefs. It is our own unhealed emotionality that seems to be running the show and being projected out onto others.

CHAPTER 3

Lessons That Were Mine to Learn

The only way out is through the darkness of our emotional memories where the pain resides. We hide behind masks seeking to control our external environment in order not to deal with our pain. As the pain rises, we cover it with more acceptable emotions such as anger or belligerence, until we can get somewhere quiet to feel our true emotions of heartache and sadness. We try all kinds of things to cope with the pain in our hearts, except to deal directly with the source of the pain.

Many of us have heard it before, but the real antidote to the pain that we experience is "true" forgiveness of self and others. The reason this antidote seems to lack effectiveness is because we are short circuiting the process, often forgiving people way too soon, before we have had a chance to express all of our rage and anger. In addition, we are trying to bring closure to situations before we get deep enough into the analysis to find our own "contribution to the chaos".

Instead of dealing with all aspects of some situation that caused us pain, we opt to project an unloving heart towards the ones we perceive as having hurt us. In order to completely forgive others, we need to forgive them as well as ourselves for "abdicating responsibility". In this way, our efforts at forgiveness can go deep enough to allow us to become clear channels for pure love.

In spiritual life coaching, we were taught to "own all of who we are". We learn to accept that we are everything which means we are the bullies… we are the intimidators… we are the victimizers…we are all things negative. This concept also means we are the harmonizers… we are the brilliant ones… we are the compassionate ones… we are all things positive. In order to become emotionally authentic, we need to own and balance all of our emotions. Let's look at some situations where I had some lessons that were mine to learn in order to further explain how to arrive at authentic emotionality.

I Told You… No You Didn't

Travel is one of my favorite hobbies. If there is any way I could visit a place, I was there. I really loved travel to the Caribbean. On one occasion I was offered the opportunity to room with my friend on one of my favorite Caribbean islands. I jumped at the chance because I was already planning to go with my book club to celebrate our fifth anniversary. This would give me the opportunity to extend my stay. I was hopeful this would work out. We continued to stay in touch, updating each other on the details.

As time got closer, my friend had organized some of her friends to meet on the island, just a few days ahead of my book club meeting. She asked me if I could fly in early. I told her I could fly in early, but I did "not" have extra money for a hotel room. She said that would "not" be a problem, because the hotel was already paid. I thought this was a "win-win" situation allowing me to extend my vacation. I was too excited.

The time arrived quickly for my big adventure. On a picture perfect sunny afternoon, I arrived on the island to vacation with my friend and her friends. The hotel was beautiful with lots of open walkways allowing for the warm summer breeze to circulate through the lobby. I could not believe my "good fortune". I was going to stay in this lovely place on the beach for the next three days. Leisure time was spent going to dinners and night clubs but mostly relaxing on the beach in deep conversation.

All too soon, it was time for the first part of my adventure to end as I was moving to another hotel on the island. I was in the room packing with the biggest smile on my face as I reminisced about the days spent so far. What brought me out of my reverie was the sound of the telephone ringing loudly. When I answered, my friend was on the other line asking me to come down to the front desk immediately. After I hung up, I could not imagine what could be wrong since I was careful not to charge anything to the room.

Soon after I arrived in the lobby, my friend quickly pulled me away from the mahogany front desk to tell me that our room was "not" paid for in advance! The pit in my stomach was so strong it felt like someone had just punched me. Have you ever had one of those moments? I reminded her she told me before we left the U.S. that I did "not" have to worry about payment for the room.

I was not prepared for her answer which was, "I never told you that"! What kind of horror show am I in? As we continued the argument, I told her she did tell me that because there was no way I would have come early since I could "not" afford to pay for extra nights in a hotel because of my hotel obligations for my book club meeting.

We went back and forth in this discussion for a while because my friend was requesting payment for the "entire" room and not just my share. Because of the miscommunication, I finally agreed to temporarily pay for the room but told her I would need reimbursement when we got back. Totally irate and full of rage, I went to the front desk to settle up the room charges for a room I did not need in the first place. With a heavy heart, I still had to stay on the island for several more nights, switch hotels, and still participate in my book club meeting. Good thing I had great members in my book club, so this incident was quickly forgotten as I continued to have fun in the sun.

When I got back home to the U.S., my first telephone call was to my friend to deal with this unresolved hotel situation. When we finally got a chance to talk, she maintained that she had told me in advance that she did "not" have money to pay for the hotel room, but that I could come and stay with her if I wanted to pay for the hotel. The story had now changed completely leaving me in doubt of any hope in recovering any of my funds. For weeks, I did not speak to my friend.

In the silence of this break in communication, I took the time to think about what was really going on. As a spiritual life coach, I have learned to ask myself in times of crisis or conflict, "What was I really upset about?" What belief was I holding which made this situation possible? After getting beyond projecting my anger onto her, I found that I was really upset because of my own belief that "I could get something for nothing". Oh!!! Did I just say that out loud? So much for me being a "good person" in this situation.

As I continued thinking back on this situation, I felt there was another belief that I was holding that allowed me to pay the "entire" hotel bill instead of just half. Why would I put myself in the position of being fully responsible? In my quiet moments, the answer that came from deep within me was not what I was expecting. I grew up believing I had to be "responsible for the irresponsible ones" especially when it came to household chores. This feeling of "total responsibility" for others carried over into adulthood. I am sure I am not the only one who has tried to help someone and at times been left holding the bag for someone else's bad decision?

In short, I was so busy looking forward to my own pleasure that I missed all of the signs that said this trip was going to be a disaster. In reflection, I could now see how the arrangements for the trip had changed several times. I ignored that, because I knew I was already going to the island and selfishly wanted to extend my stay, at no cost to me. As I continued to see where and how I abdicated responsibility for myself, it became easier for me to forgive my friend. In healing our broken hearts, we must first express our rage and anger at the source of our upset before we can see the darkness within ourselves.

Nothing Lasts Forever

As I reflected back on this situation, I thought about a statement often attributed to Maya Angelou, "When people show you who they are the first time...believe them"! Well, I can say when I heard the statement it went ignored as I gave more and more chances to my friend to show up differently. It's funny I wanted her to show up differently without changing anything about myself. So whose ego is now involved?

When we travel the same road as people with similar beliefs, it never dawns on us that there would come a time of separation. Many of us struggle with relationships that have long outgrown their mutual benefit but we stay anyway. Our hope is that someday we can rekindle the magic that was once there. In reality life goes forward never backward, so no matter how hard we wish or how deep seated our desire, there comes a point when certain friendships must end. I know this from my own experience and find it helpful to share that story with you here.

In March 2009, I made a conscious decision to pursue the oneness with God. Although I did not expect it, I found myself drifting away from a spiritual friendship I had had for more than 10 years. My friend was more than a friend; she was a spiritual mentor and a sister on my spiritual journey despite our miscommunication in the islands. Over the years, there were times we would talk for hours about the importance of God and the need to be in alignment with God's purpose for our lives. We shared our faults and our failings with each other, trusting the other to keep our confidence. How can this kind of friendship be a casualty on my road to spiritual awakening? Isn't this the kind of friendship God would put in my path to last forever? No matter what I thought, it was not to be the case.

Shortly after my father died in January 2010, I found myself pulling back and becoming more introspective about the meaning of life. Death of a "love one" has a way of doing that. During this time, whenever I wanted to share my innermost thoughts with my friend, she often had other priorities. I reached a point where I did not have the energy to pursue communication with her, instead just pulled further back. To my surprise, this lack of communication was "not" met with outreach on the part of my friend but "total silence".

At first I felt angry, but as time went on, I found myself preferring the silence which allowed clearer communication between me and God. It was from this place that I began to see the friendship in a whole new light. Using my spiritual life coaching techniques, I uncovered some of my limiting beliefs I had overlaid onto this friendship.

As I continued with the question, "What belief was I holding which kept this relationship together"? The surprising answer was "my needs do not matter". As has been said before, our beliefs create our reality. With that in mind, I unknowingly set the stage for the separation that was to come. When we have shadow or limiting beliefs, we are often unconscious of their impact on our relationships. All we know is we have trials and tribulations but we don't understand the root cause of that experience. I now suspected my root cause which would soon be validated.

We connected one last time in person as our infrequent conversations led to the suggestion that we get together. Since I was on my spiritual journey and things in my life were falling apart, I told her I did "not" have sufficient funds to travel to see her. She heard me clearly as she offered to buy me an airline ticket to come for a visit. I was so excited at this turn of events. Maybe this friendship could be saved after all. I looked forward to having fun in another city.

When I arrived to my destination, the sun was bright and the weather was warm. We picked up some fish platters then sat in the park eating and laughing like old times. In that moment, I was not sure what had separated us. I was quickly awakened from my revelry, when she said she had to go to run some errands. I asked if we could return to the park another time while I was there because the weather was going to be exceptionally beautiful over the next few days. She agreed that would be possible.

Instead of returning to the park, no matter how many times I asked, it became apparent that I was just an appendage to her life. I found myself providing ongoing support for her as she went about her daily life. I never saw another day at the park as a matter of fact I never went outside again over the next few days unless it was to run some errands or catch my flight back home. It was clear now to me how come we had drifted apart. It was in this moment I realized the relationship was permanently changed.

Once I returned home, again there was very little communication between us. Although it did not seem like a lot of time had passed between conversations, days turned into months which quickly turned into a year of not speaking. No harsh words were ever said that created this kind of separation, it's just the effort on both of our parts was lacking. It is funny how you can go from engaging daily with someone, whom you feel you could not live without, to having that person vanish from your reality in a seamless fashion. Ironically once they vanish from your reality, it is almost as if they never existed.

In the silence, an important revelation came to me. I realized now that I made my friend my link to God. Now I had a direct connection and was unwilling to let her play that role for me again. I believe it is important to join in spiritual community with other like-minded individuals. However, how many of us look to others, as I had done, for them to be our "demi-gods" seeking their approval or recommendations as to how we should live our lives?

As Christmas approached, this is always a time for self-reflection and reconciliation. I decided to send a Christmas card to my friend to thank her for the time we walked the same spiritual path together and to wish her well on her spiritual journey. I did not send the card with the expectation she would call me, but I sent a card as a way of bringing closure to a chapter that had no more words. I was surprised to hear from her. It turns out that she was looking for me at the same time I was looking for her.

In reality, I was not the same person she last talked to, nor was she the same person I last talked to. By the time we actually spoke to each other, this difference was confirmed. To me, her speech pattern was different with an air of formality and a touch of resistance and hesitancy. It did not take long for a lot of blame to surface which needed to be expressed on both our parts. As these emotions were released, there seem to be a calm that replaced the tension. When she asked the question, "Where do we go from here"? My answer was, "I really don't know". With both of us feeling fully self-expressed, we ended the conversation. To me the friendship was now in God's hands.

As a New Year rolled in, I was guided to call my friend and wish her a "Happy New Year". I thought she would call me back to tell me she received my message but I never heard from her. I was not available when she called a couple of weeks later, so she left a message on my voicemail. The message was "not" about my New Year's Day message to her but a new request to do her a "favor".

Ironically, in our last conversation, one of my chief complaints was that she frequently wanted to use my resources for her purposes. As far as I was concerned, this latest request continued to fit the pattern. I decided "not" to respond to her request immediately but to wait until we could talk again to clarify my position. I had gotten busy with other projects and forgot about the call for a few days.

As had become the pattern of late, a few days turned into a few weeks which turned into a few months which turned into never receiving another call from her. When I think about my friend now, there is much love and appreciation in my heart for the times that we spent together. However, I also now understand the relationship we had is over. As hard as it might be to move on alone, it is made easier because I know I am being guided by God.

Sometimes we have people in our lives that are constraining our ability to grow and develop. When we first meet them, they have much to share. But, as we walked the same path together absorbing what it is they have come to teach us, there comes a time when their presence becomes more of a ceiling than a floor. It is in those times, we must find the courage to separate ourselves as we remember there is nothing more important than our oneness with God.

What's Love Got to Do with It?

We get into patterns of relationships with others because the pattern is something we are familiar with. For instance, some of us find ourselves in emotionally abusive situations, because somewhere along the line emotional abuse was what we associated with love. In our conscious minds we recognize "love is not abuse". However, in our subconscious minds there is a lot of confusion because something loving at one moment can turn into something very horrible in the next. Since the mind cannot reconcile these opposing variables that quickly; some of the facts tend to get omitted in our minds to allow us the ability to continue participating in these dysfunctional relationships.

I experienced such a relationship so I know first-hand of what I speak. I had just graduated from college and was privileged to meet a corporate executive. I was mesmerized by all of her trappings of success such as a luxury car and a beautiful home in the suburbs. I looked at these "symbols of success" believing she had some wisdom to share with me. What I couldn't quite reconcile was how wonderful my friend would treat me, but after a few drinks she would turn very nasty and ugly. I was unwilling to admit to myself for a long time that she might have a problem with alcoholic based on my experiences with her.

As many of us do with those we come to love, we justify bad behavior. We mistake "love" as the cycle of "abuse then apologies" because we believe all a person really needs is "unconditional love" to change their behavior. At that time, I just believed people had flaws but it was my responsibility to work around them. I was just supposed to accept the bad behavior because that is what people do who love each other. Isn't that right?

One memory is very vivid and happened during a conversation over a glass of champagne. You see this was not the first glass of champagne we had that evening. I slowed my drinking after the first bottle but, my friend continued to drink until she opened her third bottle of champagne! Whenever my friend drank this much, she would get belligerent or aggressive which was always my clue to exit. However, this particular evening she decided to follow me to my room as I got up so she could "tell me a few things about myself"! Unfortunately, I was a guest in her house at that time and was not about to leave in the middle of the night.

In a negative and angry tone, she began telling me how I was "worthless, useless and a complete waste of her time" as I would "never amount to anything". On and on she went with her voice increasing in intensity. In my mind, I could not believe I had just brought a plane ticket to visit her just to be talked to like this. My concern now was spending another three days with her. What was I thinking when I made these reservations? Maybe I should consider incurring penalties to change my ticket?

As she continued to yell at me, there was a part of me that was so detached and very calm almost as if she was unable to reach me. I smiled from time to time which made her even angrier. In my conscious mind, I knew her comments were not aimed at me but instead she was "projecting" because she often repeated statements which were directed at her when she was a child. Whenever I tried to interrupt her tirade, she grew angrier unleashing a new round of rage.

Many questions were swirling around in my head. What is wrong with her? Why does she have to unload such ugliness on me, when I did nothing to deserve this? Suddenly she finished yelling at me and abruptly walked out of the bedroom slamming the door behind her. I sat there in the dark with this surreal feeling. The next day, she acted like that incident never happened. I did not bring it up for fear it would trigger the same bizarre behavior. How often do we tippy-toe around the bad behavior of others rather than confront them?

With this on-going behavior, part of my soul was beginning to feel constrained as anger and resentment were starting to build within me, while all the time pretending her bad behavior did not affect me. I soon learned there is no way to engage with people who are emotionally abusive, then pretend nothing is happening to your very soul. At some point, this pattern of abuse has to be interrupted. I finally realized the way people speak to me has everything to do with how I see myself.

Despite my academic accomplishments and international travel, I came to understand through my study of spiritual life coaching that my need to be loved and accepted anchored me in such a way that it created a tolerance for "bad behavior". It is to this shadow belief that my friend was triggering whenever she got drunk and told me off. Little by little, I began to be a lot more sensitive to this belief and decreased my tolerance for this bad behavior. By limiting my telephone contact with her, it gave me time to heal my own heart.

Some Things Never Change

A few years later, I reconnected to this same friend believing she had mellowed with age and hopefully slowed her drinking. We were at her kitchen table having our usual glass of champagne and in deep conversation, when all of a sudden the fireworks started. I don't know what she said but whatever it was, I disagreed with it. Her reaction to my opinion was to come across the kitchen table reaching for my neck! I jumped out of my chair pushing myself quickly away from the table to avoid her grasps.

"You will never harm me again in this lifetime", I shouted!

She jumped out of her chair all the while exclaiming, "I will do anything to you that I damn well please"!!!

The physical fight was on as she took the first swing. I did my best imitation of Muhammad Ali to avoid being hit in my face. When I realized how drunk and clumsy she was, I knew this skirmish would be short lived. As I continued to avoid her swinging at me, she remained adamant that she had the "power and control" and could do anything to me she wanted. Finally, I caught her arm in midair and held it firm. Due to her slight frame, it didn't take much for me to use my strength to bring her arm down to her side. While squeezing her forearm, I agreed only to let it go if she would stop swinging at me with her hand that was in a cast. When she calmed down, I let her go.

She promptly explained that her "head hurt" then headed straight for her bedroom.

The next morning when she made her way to the brightly lit kitchen, she asked me what had happened to her arm because she had bruises she could not explain. I told her the story of our fight and looked at her arm. To my surprise, the bruises on her arm were my fingerprints which came from me squeezing her arm very tightly to avoid being hit by her. It scared and saddened me she had no recollection of the incident.

She had probably suffered what is known as a "blackout" which is often associated with alcoholics who drink so much it impairs their recollection of events while inebriated. We discussed for a moment her behavior and tendency to get very angry and aggressive when she drinks. She brushed off my comments then fixed herself a mimosa (champagne and orange juice). Some things never change, but I needed to make a change. I decided to permanently step away from this 20 year friendship.

Victims vs. Victimizers

In hindsight it is always useful to ask the spiritual life coaching question, "What belief was I holding that made this situation possible?" As I thought for a moment, I realized I believed "love would be enough to change my friend's behavior". My human definition of "love" allowed for tolerance of verbal abuse. However, the bigger issue was that I never stopped to question for a moment, if my friend even wanted to change. In discussing my belief system with my older sister, she brought up the concept of "victimizer vs. victim".

My sister viewed many of the characteristics of my friend as those of a "victimizer" who sought to control others. She went on to say this control of another's behavior, resources, time, money or affection feed the victimizers "sense of entitlement" undergirding their ego. Since victimizers tend to generate authority, they attract people who follow them seeking to be kept "safe" in an uncertain world. The problem comes when the victim seeks to change the victimizer. This shift in power is often initiated by the victim so more of their needs can be met.

According to my sister, you cannot change a victimizer with "love" or "nagging", because victimizers fundamentally do "not" want to change since their needs are being met at the expense of others. The only way to deal with a victimizer my sister said is to "stop volunteering to be a victim". When I asked her how she arrived at this wisdom, she admitted to being a "victimizer".

CHAPTER 4

Escaping the Ego's Bad Behavior

I shared the previous stories to give you an understanding of the emotional toll we pay when we don't "escape the ego's bad behavior". By our lack of action, we are actually teaching people their ego driven behavior is acceptable. For instance, staying in the relationship with my friend with a drinking problem despite how she behaved, gave her permission to continue to treat me in a disrespectful manner. Of course, I verbalized all of the usual phrases to get her to change her behavior including phrases such as: "I don't like that", "you need to stop that", "you shouldn't talk to me like that", or "I think you are an alcoholic".

Despite making those statements, I never threatened her with the loss of our friendship. In effect there were no consequences or incentives for her to change her behavior. There was no perceived threat to her ego's bad behavior. By virtue of continuing to drink with her, I nullified my verbal statements of wanting her behavior to change. Be aware, it's not what you say that counts, but what you do about what you say that matters.

Justifying Bad Behavior

Some of us believe we are "too spiritual" to display anger or resentment at someone who mistreats us, for we are trying to live out our spiritual principles of "*turn the other cheek*". While you may appear to be accomplishing this in your external environment, you are building anger and resentment in your internal world as you deny your authentic emotionality.

In order to bring forward the kingdom of God, we must take a stand against the darkness. Now is the time for all of us to stop the justification of bad behavior, which is only allowed to exist because it is driven by "easing God out" (ego). There should be no mitigating circumstances or justification for allowing someone to be physically, emotionally or sexually abusive.

Where did I come up with the erroneous belief that God was testing my compassion in situations of repeated verbal abuse? I decided a "loving" God would "not" do such a thing. It was really the ego of the intimidator causing the bad behavior. In the moment of committing abuse, this person is totally separate from God. It is time for us to stand in our own truth, being fearless as to the consequences which can be imposed by another.

Ironically to move into oneness with ourselves means we must become selfish and set boundaries with others acting with disrespect in our world. What gets done to us is because we are "allowing" it by holding beliefs which make certain situations possible. We are choosing to feed our "life force energy" into the very relationships that seem to be holding us in bondage.

Being Responsible for the Irresponsible Ones

When I was growing up, many of our parents believed in disciplining children according to a "peer accountability model". At least that is what I call it. In this way of disciplining children, each child is made accountable for the behavior of the others. Whenever any bad decisions were made which went against the parent's instructions, then all of the children were equally punished. In this model, confusion was created because of the unwillingness of the offending party to admit to guilt.

The conversations often went like… "I am not telling"… "but you have too"… "No, I don't "… but we will be punished"… "So, I don't care". This led to my limiting belief of feeling "responsible for the irresponsible ones". To avoid punishment, I often tried to control the behavior of my sisters. Don't get me wrong, this strategy was not altruistic for the benefit of them but for my own self- protection.

As a young adult, I found myself continuing to magnetizing to me experiences that would often make me the victim. Whenever I complained about the unfairness, I was frequently met with the comment, "What's the big deal"? This was the one phrase I hated hearing growing up because it made me feel so powerless. If you wanted to see me really boiling mad then do something negative to me followed by the remark "What's the big deal"? Why is it people believe they can pursue their selfish desires, without any thought as to the impact on others then blame others for getting in the way of their pursuits?

As I reached middle age, I thought I had outgrown the shadow belief of "being responsible for the irresponsible ones". However, this limiting belief reared its head on a multimillion dollar contract I was managing. Unconscious limiting beliefs can follow you for many years if unhealed, reaching into the highest levels of success. In this case, I was very good at providing outstanding reports to my clients but this became my "Achilles Heel".

I ran into a problem with substandard reporting by one of my subcontractors which was beyond my capacity to dramatically alter due to the technical nature of the information. When I discussed this situation with the client, I was told "fix it". I then discussed this lack of adequate reporting with the subcontractor who then said "we don't do reports, we just do the work". This statement was followed by the dreaded words, "What's the big deal"?

Well the big deal was payment for services rendered depended upon the adequacy of the report writing. I went back and forth with the subcontractor trying to get more information into the reports that would allow for an understanding of what had been accomplished that month.

When I chatted again with the client about this lack of information, the client again told me to "fix it". So now I had to spend extra time reviewing the short report and expanding it where I could as a way to compensate for the lack of reporting. I was once again "responsible for the irresponsible ones". When will this end? Once again I felt total resentment at having this experience again.

It was two years after the contract ended that I was able to see my contribution to the chaos. What belief was I holding that allowed this situation to perpetuate itself? The belief was I felt "responsible for the irresponsible ones". Instead of submitting to the client what was provided by the subcontractor, I thought it should be altered. I made a decision instead of taking the consequences for the substandard reporting.

To change the pattern, I would have to get passed fearing punishment for the deeds of another. Until we are clear about the limiting beliefs motivating and driving our behaviors, we will continue to experience similar situations which generate similar emotions such as anger and upset within us.

Getting Out of the Loop

How do we get to the point where we have the memories but not the emotions of our past history? The first thing we must do is to admit to the level of pain and hurt still residing within from those experiences. For most of us, while the experience was happening, we were constrained from fully expressing our true emotionality because we were often angry with authority figures that we were also dependent upon. As a result there is "residual emotionality" built up that has never been released.

It is this residual emotionality that the ego uses to stay vigilant against similar circumstances. Due to the "law of attraction", instead of being free from similar experiences, we often magnetize similar experiences. No matter how vigilant you appear to be, it always seems you become "victimized" when you least expect. So, how do we get out of this loop that the ego has us anchored in?

One of the things that keep us stuck in this way of seeing reality is we think as individuals we see the entire picture. It is only our own arrogance that does not acknowledge what we actual see is simply a "fragmented view of reality". The reason this view is fragmented is because we are seeing through our ego which is primarily concerned with self-preservation and therefore cannot consider the impact of any decisions as others would see it.

In addition, since our arrogance has us believing that what we see is what is "true", then our decisions are made with the belief that anybody who opposes us is not seeing "the truth". We are deluding ourselves if we think without divine guidance we can produce outcomes that will be equally beneficial for everybody. If we let our ego be our guide, then we must be mindful of the expression, "what you see, depends on where you sit".

Be mindful of your "ego speak" so you limit your arrogance and aggressiveness aimed at dominating the outcome. You must get yourself to the point where you can honestly say, "You don't know what needs to happen in this situation". If you can bring yourself to admit "nothing that you see means anything" then you are making room for God to work through you.

Sometimes, we can get so caught up in our ego view of our own innocence to the point where we cannot see our "contribution to the chaos". This is a good time to remember even Jesus is reported to have said *"none is good but the father."* Once we can see our own "darkness within" then we will understand how this perception of reality has led us to "wrong thinking" which has led us to "display our own bad behavior".

We should keep in mind that "bad behavior" is not a result of being a "bad person" but is often attributed to having a distorted perception of reality upon which to base our decisions. When we get to that place where we have resolved our own emotional issues, we will not hold others in bondage to their bad decisions. Just this little shift in our thinking will allow us to show compassion and understanding for the misbehavior of others.

We must be mindful for at times what we think of as someone else's bad behavior is often a reflection of our own. We tend to focus on the bad behavior of others because it is a way to deflect from our responsibility in the drama. If we look deeper, we are usually angry because we have "abdicated responsibility" for ourselves.

This way of being triggers guilt within yourself because you did not do something you were supposed to do, instead you left decisions about yourself to other people who took advantage of you. Your full anger has been projected out onto them as opposed to owning your bad decision for abdicating responsibility for yourself.

This projection of your emotions is one of the ego's greatest weapons because it allows you to project your guilt onto others. If you don't acknowledge and then release your guilt, it will continue to hold you prisoner to your ego. The way out is through. You must withdraw your complaints from others for their failure to meet your demands because if you don't, you will feel you have justification for attack. It is this attack that keeps us separate and apart from one another. If we have anger and hatred in our hearts towards one another then we cannot be in the oneness with God.

We must de-escalate our need to have our individual desires reign over the needs of everyone and everything. It is this selfish way of being which is creating the emotional torment that continues to leave us all unhappy and dissatisfied. The more desires we have which are thwarted the more limiting beliefs get created taking us further away from the ability to live life with an open heart.

In order to stay authentic in your emotionality, whenever you encounter situations where you have a negative or lower vibrational response, the question for you is, "What belief am I holding that makes this situation possible"? Do not focus your attention in times of chaos or confusion on the bad behavior of others, for everything that you are seeing is being magnetized into your experience because of your shadow beliefs. It is imperative you understand your internal belief system in order to change your external environment. Under whose control is your internal thought system...ego or God? The experience you are having will tell you.

Many of us believe our thoughts are being guided by God but in reality even the "good" thoughts can be nothing more than the "light side" of our ego. We somehow believe if we have "good intentions" as spiritual beings then our actions should be accepted by those we are trying to help. However, unless you have healed the "walking wounded" part of your emotionality, you become nothing more than an "unhealed healer" contributing to confusion you are seeking to resolve.

As spiritual beings we must be conscious of our arrogance and our righteous positions which are grounded in the conditioning we receive in our cultures. If your residual emotionality has not been cleared, then your ego will always find a place to hide making it difficult for you to be a "clear channel for God's use". For those on the spiritual path, there may come a time when you may have to press "pause" from the studying of spiritual philosophy in favor of "living" an authentic life. As you climb out of the darkness within, the only thing left will be the light in alignment with your spiritual philosophy.

It is time for the "rubber to hit the road" as those on the spiritual path effortlessly live these spiritual principles sharing love, tolerance and patience with one another. Open up your minds, open up your hearts, open up your lives to fully embrace your authentic emotionality for therein is your pathway to God. As you align your feeling nature with God's guidance then you will no longer feel the need to reflect upon your past or control your future. This leaves you in the only time that matters…now.

Are You Really Personally Responsible?

As we try to escape the ego's bad behavior we can only do it by embracing our authentic emotionality. If there is anger, sadness, hostility or rage which needs to be expressed, then vent it. Once you have fully expressed your emotions, you are more likely to be objective regarding your "contribution to the chaos". This brings us to another spiritual life coaching concept "personal responsibility". Many of us think of ourselves as personally responsible since we have jobs, pay bills, take care of our families, and honor God.

If someone were to ask you if you are being personally responsible, your answer would most definitely be "yes". But I beg to differ, because most of us don't even realize what "personal responsibility" really is. How many times in the last week, have you said to someone, "Look what you made me do" or "You get on my nerves"? If you have used these phrases then according to spiritual life coaching, you are "not" being personally responsible. I can hear you now saying…What???

In spiritual life coaching, personal responsibility means "you do not blame anybody for any decision you make or any action you take, never claiming your emotional reactions are based on someone else's behavior". Now I ask you again, do you still think of yourself as "personally responsible"? This concept when first introduced to me and others seems impossible to master. How do you live your life not blaming anybody for things they are doing which upset you "causing your reactions"? The goal of this book is to make you aware of the obstacles which block you from oneness with God, self, and others.

As you saw from my situations, you could say I was "not" taking personal responsibility as I blamed each of my friends for their treatment of me which I thought "caused" my anger. In truth, my anger was internal because I "abdicated responsibility" for myself which caused my shame and guilt which got projected out as anger towards them. We must own our own bad behavior completely before we can see what bad behavior others should be held accountable for.

Newsflash, we are not here to serve the "ego of man" but we are here to build the "kingdom of God". I make it a conscious practice to no longer serve the ego of man. If you want to interact with me, my requirement is that you operate from a place of oneness with God. In desiring something from me, it has to be done in such a way that I can feel God's presence in your request.

If God is not at the center of your being when you make a request, the benefit will be only to you and I will feel resistance to the request. It is now rare for me to override this resistance to honor your request because it will put me out of alignment with my own spirit. I am very reluctant to move myself out of alignment with the spirit of God within me just to satisfy someone else's ego desires. I am encouraging you to do the same, to stand in your truth, to "just say no".

Creating Boundaries

At this point in the reading, you may be thinking to yourself that I seem to be advocating a level of selfishness and disinterest in other people and their problems. "Yes", I am saying that. It is time to begin to separate yourself from the needs, wants, and desires of other people so you can create more room to access your authentic self.

Without proper boundaries you cannot escape the grasps of someone's ego because you have tied your hearts desires to someone else's ego desires which can never fully be satisfied. You cannot become authentic as long as you continue to make decisions that prioritize everybody else's wants above your own.

What is helpful in this situation is for you to withdraw from the demands of others and retreat into the quiet stillness. In the silence, you can begin to get back in communion with the "essential essence" of who God made you to be. This way of being is often not possible in the fast moving, quick acting society we live in.

We have taken on so many beliefs and behaviors which are not our own but were really imposed upon us from childhood. We tolerated these things because we had no other choice as others held authority over us at that time. However if you are reading this book, I can assure you whatever authority was held over you is no longer in effect.

You are absolutely old enough now to "release yourself from your past" instead of spending the rest of your life reacting to what somebody did to you when you were 5, 10, 15 or 20. Unfortunately, these old patterns and painful memories tend to control our current behavior. It is time we challenge these old patterns and beliefs.

CHAPTER 5

Reconciling the Darkness Within

One of the reasons we are unable to live our spiritual beliefs while adhering to our authentic emotionality is because we have real life experiences which tend to run contrary to what we learn in religious institutions. For instance, in church we are taught to "*turn the other cheek*" but in our hearts at times, we really want to "knock someone out". How do we reconcile these two different ways of thinking? Many of us opt to value what is "good" and what is "moral", but focusing on these alone will not bring you into oneness with God. It is a good start, but it's not enough because what separates you from God and others is the darkness that is within yourself.

The Only Way Out is Through

It is important to first acknowledge the darkness within you because the only way out is through. You have had situations that created trauma in your life which built up unexpressed emotionality. If you do not release yourself from this unexpressed emotionality, you will continue to project it out onto others. That projection will cause others to react to you in a certain way with you unaware of the situation you are creating. Life is not happening to you, life is a result of decisions you have made. In order to live the life God intended, we must be conscious of the world you are creating. At this point, you may be asking, "How can you say that what I am experiencing I have created"?

There are many spiritual disciplines which discuss the "law of attraction" and other concepts which distort our perception. One of these books that I have read at least three times is a book entitled "A Course in Miracles". The early pages of the workbook of "A Course in Miracles" make reference to such concepts as "nothing that we see means anything because we give everything all the meaning that it has". It goes on to comment about our unhealed emotions which act as filters bringing up past memories to distort our current reality.

Each of us has had traumatic experiences in life that have moved us from a place of pure love to a place of fear. Because of this distortion, we tend to process information from our reality in a very fragmented way using our outdated "frame of reference". What I see and how I react may no longer be appropriate to the current situation. Let me give you an example using a real life situation from my sister.

If I were to go into a store, and see a group of youth who were talking loudly, I would not have much of a reaction. However my older sister, whenever she had such encounters, she would get very fearful. Why the difference in reactions? In my life coaching session with my sister, I asked her that question to get an understanding about why loud talking youth bothered her so much. She said she did not know but would do her "homework" by writing about her true feelings and let me know. She came back to me the next day with her observations. She said her fearful reaction to youth was rooted in her painful childhood memories with gang members in Philadelphia.

My sister recounted the day she was walking home passing through "gang territory". She was only about 10 years old when a group of teenage boys sitting in a nearby park started talking loudly threatening to "beat her up". My sister said her reaction was to pretend she did not hear them, so she didn't run but continued to walk at the same pace.

Despite this external perception of calm and defiance, her heart was beating very fast. Nothing happened to her because of her perceived "fearlessness". However, it was from that experience almost 45 years later she continued having negative reactions to groups of loud talking teenage youth.

After doing her homework and releasing the unexpressed emotionality, it ended her need to react in these types of situations.

Ending the Shadow Boxing With Our Past

I share this story to say all of us are "shadow boxing" with our past. All of us are projecting onto others unresolved situations which really don't even involve them. We are reacting to perceived stimulus trying to be proactive in stopping it before any potential hurt can be inflicted. It is time for us to deal with what life is showing us…about us. It is time for us to understand our own triggers which generate our emotional responses. It is time for us to go deep within our own being to reconcile the darkness within.

Each of us has painful memories from experiencing the underbelly of the darkness that humanity has heaped upon us including: betrayal, abandonment, manipulation, intimidation, victimization and more. It is from these experiences that we have created certain shadow or limiting beliefs that continue to give our external environment control over our behavior. The solution to handling emotional triggers which cause us to shadow box with our past is to deactivate the trigger instead of trying to control the external environment.

How do you deactivate the trigger? The first thing you must do is to recognize that triggers are real. In taking personal responsibility for your feelings you allow yourself to recognize when something upsets you, frustrates you, creates fear in you, or makes you unhappy. From the recognition of the trigger you can begin your own assessment seeking to uncover potential patterns to your reactions as well as your "contribution to the chaos".

Start by asking yourself the question, "Where has this happened to me before"? You will get an answer because what is happening to you now has probably happened to you before. What pattern is being revealed? Accessing the pattern allows you to focus on the trigger which needs to be addressed as was shown in the previous example.

For it is only in releasing the unexpressed emotionality in the heart that triggers can then be neutralized. Once emotional triggers are dealt with the corresponding beliefs can be shifted allowing for permanent changes to your behavior to be possible. Trying to change your behavior without addressing your triggers in your heart space will provide short-term success but long-term failure.

Engaging Our Hearts

Many of us believe we can simply change our minds which will change our behavior. Nothing could be further from the truth. We can change our minds but life is not an intellectual exercise. We must begin now to reengage our hearts in our decision-making process. The problem is many of us are afraid of what is in our hearts. The heart I am talking about is the "intuitive place of feeling" not the emotional place of reaction to external triggers.

Without your heart engaged, you will continue to make decisions from an ego-centric perspective without the proper understanding of your impact on other people. To live in oneness with each other, we must make decisions that are beneficial to all. How can we make a decision that is beneficial to someone else when we are so disconnected from our own hearts and our own divine impulses?

In trying to become emotionally authentic, we must look at our contribution to the chaos. When things happen, most of the time we blame others for our emotional reactions. We just talked about personal responsibility. I cannot stress enough that we are no longer victims of the world we see, we are actually creating the world we see through our own beliefs. Whatever we are doing which causes someone else to be triggered is their responsibility. The reaction and bad behavior we are displaying is our responsibility.

We must try and get to a place where we are able to be neutral in our reactions to another person's bad behavior allowing more tolerance for people to work out their own spiritual evolution. We have to allow for the uniqueness of individuals to be okay with us without trying to change people into carbon copies of ourselves to meet our ego demands.

Most of the conflict and chaos we engage in comes from a place of judgment not a heartfelt place. Ironically, our judgment comes from a distorted view of reality. The closer you get to your own center, the more you realize that what happens to others is not for you to make different because you do not know what experiences will benefit others on their spiritual path. Each one of us is connected to the spirit of God who knows what each person needs to experience to move into spiritual alignment.

For those of us who are continually having conflict and chaos, be mindful of dealing with life from a "victimization consciousness" not fully connected to the essential essence of who God made us to be. In lacking that connection to our divine self, we are lacking a permanent connection to God that is powerful. It is not God who has gone anywhere; it is just that we are choosing not to connect to God's infinite power and wisdom because "we think we know". It is our own arrogance dominated by our ego that is creating the chaos and conflict we are experiencing in our world. It is our own ego that is masterminding the confusion of our lives. It is time to take your ego out of the driver's seat.

Accessing Deep Seated Emotionality

You must access those places within yourself where you still feel hurt and pain. It is in our heart where the pain can create darkness to which the ego structure can anchor itself. It is not enough to say daily affirmations, set intentions, take action steps, or do what is "right" or "good". It's not enough because the pain that is in your heart when it is unexpressed acts like anchors on your feet pulling you down into the darkness. The way to elevate your consciousness, the way to move yourself out of this way of being, is to access and open up your heart to allow it to feel again.

Many of us will not allow our hearts to truly feel again because of the ego damage that has been done to us by others. You will have to see your mother, father, guardian or caretakers in a new light. People who cared for you were also affected by the bad behavior of others. Some of the bad behavior that has shaped your life may not have been done intentionally but nevertheless it was done.

In order to reach your authentic emotionality you must accept the dark emotions that will rise when you think about your past. Not everything that happened to you when you were a child was because of something you did that required authority to behave as it did. Much of what guides our behaviors today is not what we did when we knew better, it is more what someone else did to us. It is this pattern that needs to be interrupted as we seek to bring ourselves into emotional authenticity. There is no way to be one with another if in your memory lies a wounded heart from mistreatment.

Accessing my authentic emotionality finally came together in a really surprising way. As I spent more time in sharing my spiritual life coaching skills with others, I became more aware of my own emotional authenticity. One of the things I learned about myself was that I was never really okay with the way others were treating me but I was more horrified by uncovering my own shame and guilt as I looked at my contribution to the chaos that was my life.

It was so easy to blame others on a consistent basis when things did not turn out the way I had expected. As I began to withdraw my erroneous blame on others, I began to forgive. It was only in this way I could understand the saying of Jesus while hanging on the cross, "*forgive them father, for they know not what they do*".

It was not until my father died unexpectedly in 2010 that my unexpressed residual emotionality found its way to the surface. While I was at a world religion conference in Australia, I found out that my father was in the hospital in a coma in Philadelphia. A week later when I returned home, I found out the diagnosis was terminal colon cancer with a maximum of six months to live. The blessing was he came out of the coma quickly but from the time of the diagnosis to the time of his death was approximately 30 days.

Although I was blessed to still have my mother with me, I was not prepared for my father to transition in such a rapid manner during the Christmas holidays. After visiting him in the hospital a couple of times, I finally found some time to get quiet to deal with my new reality and to feel the emotions that were welling up inside of me. As can be expected the tears started to come slowly at first then in a torrent rush. I couldn't seem to stop crying.

I thought about all the great times my father and I had together. As I remembered all of our recent father-daughter "breakfast club" meetings at local restaurants, I cried even harder at the thought that would never happen again. I felt thankful and grateful I had reconciled with my father living in peace with him during his final years.

As I allowed myself to continue to really feel the sadness, it dawned on me I had never allowed myself to truly feel the depths of my sadness whenever I experienced trauma in my life. With this new awareness came more tears but what was interesting was I was no longer crying about my father. There was so much sadness within my heart I did not fully express. It was all of this unexpressed emotionality that I allowed myself to feel completely... sadness, anger, hurt and pain.

This deep seated crying went on for hours which turned into todays and ended in about one week. I woke up one morning and there just seemed to be no more tears. There was stillness within my being as I had finally reached the bottom of my own soul. What kept me from reaching the core essence of myself before now was my unwillingness to go into the darkness of my own pain. It is the darkness within that binds us, inhibiting us from reaching the light.

It's Not That Bad

The health consequence of suppressing our emotionality is the last thing I would like to address in this section. Quite often when we are going through difficult emotional times, we continue to tell ourselves "it is not that bad." I don't know whether we truly believe it or if we tell ourselves this so we can somehow get through it.

For me during emotionally difficult times, I tried to keep my emotions in check by relying extensively on sugars to elevate my mood and allow me to keep moving. Whenever there was a problem, I would eat something like pudding, cake, pie, or ice cream that instantly made me feel better as it activated my serotonin levels which elevated my mood. I was fairly active so my body did not reflect this terrible habit.

As you continue to read my story, think about how you cope with situations that are "not that bad". Most of us believe we can go through life, without being completely authentic in our emotional expressions yet have no consequences to our physical body. This is a fallacy to which unfortunately I am living proof. To most people I seemed like a happy, kind, giving sort of personality which for the most part is true. However, I also tend to internalize my problems, negativity, and difficult decisions. It is this internalizing of negative emotionality that would eventually play havoc on my body.

Here is an example. I agreed to meet my mother and sister at a local restaurant. We had come together as a way to find relief from the ongoing construction that my sister was going through. There was nothing unusual about our conversations, as we laughed often when we got together. When it came time to order food, I focused on a dish from the menu that included salmon, feta cheese, and salad. In my mind I thought this was a healthy choice.

However, I heard this "still small voice" say to me "order it without the cheese because of the salt in this brand of cheese". Since I was not totally in tuned with my spirit at that time, I ignored the message. I loved feta cheese and did not understand why I was being denied it. So I put in my order the way I wanted it…

When the food came, I began eating and chatting as usual. However about halfway through the meal, I was starting to feel a little sickly. As was my custom, I kept this feeling to myself. I am very in tune with my body so I can feel anything that is not right. At this point, my brain felt like fireworks were going off in it as I felt an unusual amount of tingling. I instantly heard a message, to stop eating immediately.

As I put the fork down, I felt this warm energy rise up my spine and spread across my shoulders. This warm energy turned to the left and started up my neck and as it went there was incredible tingling. As it passed the lower part of my jaw, I felt paralysis begin to settle in but the heat continued up towards my eardrum where I soon heard a pop. I felt my eyes starting to roll around in my head as I was beginning to lose consciousness. The last thing I saw were my mother and my sister laughing in conversation. In that moment, I knew I was having a "stroke".

One of the last thoughts I remembered was "not now, I cannot do this to my mother and sister, not now". In that moment, it seemed as if that thought temporarily halted the next steps in the stroke process. I could still hear the "still small voice" which was now guiding me to drink lots of ice water and absolutely pass on dessert.

As the lunchtime conversations continued, I didn't say much because I could feel the numbness on the left side of my face as I spoke. When dessert came, I absolutely did not partake because I knew with sugars came salts. As we ended our meal together and gave each other hugs. I knew I had to change my diet as well as deal better with the stress which came from covering up my authentic emotionality. For if I did not I would cease to exist.

I no longer took for granted I would wake up in the morning with everything in my body fully functional. Over time, with facial exercises, the ability to control my facial muscles returned to almost normal functioning. It took me almost a year to confirm the symptoms of this self-diagnosis with a doctor because while everything in my life was falling apart, I also did "not" have health insurance. So I did the only thing I could do; I became a lot more vigilant about diet and exercise and "baby aspirin".

I shared this story to remind everyone that burying your unhealed emotionality in food will never lead to an authentic life but will potentially lead to long term health issues. You deserve better and can have better by embracing your authentic emotionality and trusting your "divine guidance".

PART 2

Trust Divine Guidance

CHAPTER 6

Building a New Foundation

I f you are willing to trust in "divine guidance", be prepared for your life to fall apart. It is almost impossible to build your divine life upon the same foundation as your human life. In this section of the book, I will share with you aspects of my spiritual journey as I transitioned from my human self as the foundation for my decision-making.

I have come to learn problems are given to us in life because it is the only way we can evolve in "spiritual maturity" as we readjust our values in light of what is truly important. Ironically, we think we know that already, but what we too often practice is the result from our human values not our divine values. Once you answer the call to "trust divine guidance" just know you will struggle with your ability to live in "uncertainty".

Difficulty in Following Divine Guidance

What is "divine guidance"? Simply put, divine guidance means to be led by the spirit of God within you. This process is made difficult if you have not embraced your authentic emotionality, because the messages you feel you are receiving from God may be distorted as a result of your human experiences. Just by living in the "real world", we create an alternative belief system to what we learn in religious institutions.

Messages like "*trust in the Lord with all thy heart and all thy mind*" get distorted by our human experiences when we are constantly reinforced by our culture to "distrust". How can we "*lean not unto thy own understanding, but in all thy ways acknowledge him*", if we do not know how to trust?

How do we reconcile our human behaviors with our spiritual beliefs? The answer lies in pressing "pause" on your spiritual belief system long enough to allow for your very real human emotions to be fully expressed. That is why much attention was given to the topic of embracing your authentic emotionality for there is no way to trust divine guidance without first trusting the emotionality within yourself.

Many of us think we know what God wants from us. We know our talents, we know our strengths; therefore, we think we know our destiny. It is true all of us are here for a divine purpose, but how do we really know what that is? Is your divine purpose what you are doing now in your life? Is your "work life" the same as your "life's work"? The only way to find out is by being willing to let go of what you think you understand.

You have to be willing to let go of guiding your life making ego based decisions without consultation with God. Divine guidance requires you to be open to uncertainty in order to become a "clear channel for God's use". If you think you know, you restrict the ability of God to guide.

How do you know if the divine messages you are receiving are accurate? Many times we think we understand what God wants from us so we proceed to go and do. However, to our surprise the outcome is not what we expected.

One reason this happens is because there is a disconnection between what we think we "hear" and what was really "meant". The disconnection comes as a result of the distortion in the communications channel between us and God. The problem is not that God is not giving you the proper guidance. The problem is our various experiences have created a "human filter" that does not allow for us to be open to clearly hearing our divine messages.

There are many ways to receive guidance from the spirit of God within. To limit distortion, we should seek guidance from a place of stillness and silence...no radio, no television, no telephones, no computers... just complete silence. In seeking divine guidance, we must also come with an open heart and an open mind.

This is not the time to tell God what you want and how you want God to fulfill your personal agenda. This is a time to come to God in communion to allow God to fill you up with his purpose. There is much to do in our world to move us towards the oneness where we can truly share love with one another.

All of us have special gifts and talents that can be used in the building of God's kingdom on earth. However, the ability to know how your talents are to be used is not for you and you alone to decide. The way your talents are to be used is up to God who created you in the first place.

It is only God who has the total view of how each of the puzzle pieces, which are our lives, will come together. Every puzzle piece is important because the puzzle is not complete if it is missing even one part, no matter how small. Therefore, all 7 billion people on earth are God's puzzle pieces which are needed to create *"earth as it is in heaven"*. However, it is because of our human arrogance that we insist our way of seeing reality is comprehensive.

How do we open up to trusting something beyond our own egos? The answer lies in moving through the darkness within yourself in order to allow your "separate self" to dissolve into the oneness. Without a willingness to do that, then all of the spiritual messages you receive will tend to be distorted.

Unless you are willing to allow the human foundation you have created to fall apart, you will always be limited in what you can build. Most of us are seeking to increase our capacity and push the limits of our potential, however this can only be done effectively under the guidance of our "divine self" not our "ego self".

Beyond Duality

The limits on our potential are put in place by our ego which uses a structure of analysis and evaluation of variables to determine what is "good and bad" or what is "right and wrong". What happens to our lives if we no longer use this ego guidance system to make decisions? What replaces this way of thinking?

To live under the guidance of God, means to be obedient to the divine impulses which are coming from a place of oneness where all variables have already been accounted for. Only through a fundamental understanding of "who and what" God is will you then allow yourself to truly trust "something greater than yourself".

In my spiritual life, God embodies three major characteristics. God is "omnipresent" which means God is everywhere at all times within me and outside of me reflected in all of creation. God is "omniscient" which means God is all-knowing therefore I do not have to tell God what I want for God already knows the purpose and destiny of everything that has been created. God is "omnipotent" which means God has all power so there can be no opposition to the will of God. As the saying goes, *"If God is for me, who can be against me"*.

This fundamental understanding of "who and what" God is creates the foundation for my theology in which there can be no such concept as "evil being a rival power to God". Instead I see people committing "evil acts" because they have lost their connection to God. Unfortunately in this separated state, the darkness of the ego takes control of the decision-making process allowing people to be insensitive as they seek to crush, kill or destroy others. Any thought system where the ego has unlimited power in deciding reality is unreliable and easily distorted because it is based in "duality".

Let's look further at this concept of "duality" because in order to trust divine guidance, you must be willing to transcend duality. We all learn as children to distinguish between variables such as "hot and cold" or "in and out". This concept is often referred to as duality. We are taught to use our minds to interpret our reality so that we make the best decisions for ourselves.

The standards for what are the best decisions are programmed into us by a series of external variables such as parents, guardians, ethnicity, education, income and cultural norms. All of these variables form the structure into which we put new information to determine our own behavior. With our fundamental beliefs put into us by others, how do we become clear channels for God's use?

The first step in making any kind of change is awareness, for it is through awareness of a situation that change is possible. Now that you are aware your entire belief system has been created for you, adopted by you then strengthened by your own experiences. That is why it is referenced in "A Course in Miracles" that nothing we see means anything because we give everything all the meaning that it has.

Our way of seeing reality when dominated by our ego is very subjective and can be shifted in a moment's notice. For instance we are taught it is wrong to kill another human being for that is one of the "Ten Commandments" of the Bible and part of the foundation of religious traditions.

While everyone acknowledges this concept to be true, as humans we make exceptions to this rule. The exceptions to the rule include killing people in war or killing people in self-defense. So is killing people wrong or is killing people situational? Since no two people think alike or see things exactly the same, this human way of decision making is quite arbitrary. Therefore what is "good" and what is "bad" is always in the eye of the beholder.

This way of seeing reality is what allows for a morally reprehensible act like killing another human being to be deemed acceptable depending upon the situation. It is this ego way of making decisions which needs to be shifted to God's control. As we grow in spiritual maturity, we will not harm another who we then experience as an extension of ourselves.

CHAPTER 7

Letting the Rubber Hit the Road

How do we move to this place of true human connectedness? How do we transcend duality? Are these ideas even really possible? Not only are these ideas really possible, but they are inevitable. Those of us who are dedicated to a spiritual path have already tested the limits of our human capacity and have found them wanting. Therefore, we have opened ourselves up to exploring our divine self in a new way. What happens when we really "let the rubber hit the road" by living our spiritual philosophy without concern for the human consequences to ourselves? I made a conscious decision to find out and these are some of my spiritual adventures.

Have You Lost Your Mind

In March of 2009, I made the decision to terminate my consulting contract early and forgo invoicing almost $70,000 per month. I pushed for this decision because I truly believed I had "been to the mountaintop" in terms of human accomplishments. Instead of finding bliss in the "American Dream", all I found was constant conflict in my professional and personal relationships. I was making more money than I ever imagined, but there were always fights with employees and subcontractors who wanted to take some of "my money" away. I was supposed to be happy in my romantic relationship but instead I was engaged in constant conflict over spiritual rituals used to connect to God. At this point, I had enough! I was no longer motivated to set anymore intentions or achieve anymore ego based goals.

The new challenge for me was to find out, "What happens to my life if I don't guide it"? Is there really a God that will step in and take control, if I let go? The only goal now became to be one with myself, be one with others, be one with God, by allowing my divine self to lead. I was quite versed in the spiritual lingo such as "what you believe, you can achieve" or "we are co-creating our reality". I was already master of my universe because any goal I held firmly in my mind I had manifested. Some may be wondering had I lost my mind? I did not think so; I was ready to be a "spiritual adventurer" in my search for God.

I had prepared well for my journey to spiritual awakening because I had done the work on myself. I had a certification in spiritual life coaching which I used to clear "my vessel" of major repressed emotional trauma. I had studied all of the major spiritual writers of my day and saw most of them in person at conferences. I even studied all of the world's spiritual traditions beginning with my religion Christianity then moved on to studying other religious traditions including: Hinduism, Buddhism, Taoism, Islam, and Judaism. Not only did I study these spiritual philosophies, I visited 40 countries around the world such as Italy, India, Thailand, China, Egypt and Israel where these spiritual traditions were practiced.

I was now beyond the point where I wanted to read and study anything else. I was beyond wanting to be a "seeker". I was more interested in "feeling the presence of God" in my daily life. I wanted to know, "How do I live this spiritual philosophy"? How do I subjugate my ego's need to control tangible physical reality so I can become a clear channel for God's use? What would my life look like if I lived from my divine self instead of my human self? I felt I was ready to trust divine guidance, but what I was "not" ready for was for my life to fall apart.

Ready for the Spiritual Journey

As the spring of 2009 turned to summer, I could not have been happier. I was free to spend my days doing exactly as I pleased without worrying about the lack of money. Lack of money is often what stops most of us from making any changes in our lives. I was no exception to that rule. I don't believe I would have had the same courage to make changes if I had to worry about finances. But let me not get ahead of myself in the story because lack of finances ultimately becomes an issue. I spent this quiet time reading, writing, studying, and exercising in order to keep my mind, body, and spirit in perfect alignment with God. What I took away from my spiritual life coaching process and previous study of myself was the way I connected best to God was by having a very peaceful and quiet environment.

Since I was attuned to the spirit of God within me, I knew I could hear the messages given to me that confirmed I was on the right path leading to my divine self. I learned early to use my multi-sensory gifts to communicate with God. In order to receive divine messages it is important to operate beyond your five senses. Some of us admit to being "clairvoyant" because we have visions that are not in our current reality but eventually manifest. Others are considered "clairsentient" because they are able to feel emotional vibrations alerting them to problems even before knowing the details with their conscious minds. Finally there are those of us who are "clairaudient" because they are able to clearly hear the "still small voice" of the spirit of God sharing information and wisdom far beyond their conscious knowing. I am primarily clairaudient which got amplified once I calmed the chatter inside of my head. How did I calm the chatter you may ask? The path I took to quieting my mind was by embracing my authentic emotionality which has left my mind so quiet that at times, I can hear the swoosh of air hitting my eardrums.

As mentioned before in December of 2009, I was faced with an unexpected tragedy as my father was diagnosed with terminal colon cancer. It was predicted he had up to 6 months to live, but in reality, he lasted only 30 days. In my newfound spiritual walk I was not prepared for such a devastating loss, for I believed that being in alignment with God meant I would be "free from human tragedy". Nothing could have been further from the truth. After my father's funeral in January of 2010, I found myself very emotionally distraught and somewhat disillusioned by the amount of energy I put into pursuing my spiritual awakening. I was beginning to question whether it was really possible to be one with God in this dimension of reality.

Why would God take my father at this time in my life when I was preparing myself to do the will of God? I was blessed to still have my mother for emotional and financial support, but losing my father brought this new feeling of being "unprotected". No sooner had I asked this question about why my father was taken then I was guided to watch a video on the life of Jesus Christ. As I watched the movie, I got to see what I missed in watching the movie twice before. There was a scene in the movie where Jesus was talking to God after his father's death. Jesus was asking God why he would take his father's protection from him at this time in his life when God had a divine destiny for him. In that instant, I burst into tears when I realized that my father's absence created space for my dependence on God. For without complete dependence on God all I sought to accomplish on my spiritual journey would never manifest.

God's Ways Are Not Our Ways

In the spring of 2010 as I began to get my footing back under me, I understood for the first time the expression *"God's ways are not our ways"*. I had been given a great gift as I started writing my first book entitled "Awakening of a Chocolate Mystic". In trying to feel some kind of usefulness and purposefulness about my life, I decided it was time to look into publishing the book. Over the next year, I had a few people read the draft before finally submitting it for publication with Balboa Press, subsidiary of Hay House. Visions of becoming a well-known author began swirling around in my head. Many of my friends and family read the book with astonishment. Reading about my mystical experiences and spiritual philosophy allowed them to begin to see their own lives in a new light.

However, as I was beginning to find on the spiritual journey, we often tend to run ahead of God in our decision making thereby disconnecting ourselves from the "flow of the universe". As to my experience, I was so busy trying to move my book in terms of distribution, I soon found out how difficult a process it really was. As the early book sales fell off, the bills came due. Now I was starting to feel the pinch of economic uncertainty. I could not rationalize in my mind how I could be following God and experiencing economic difficulty.

CHAPTER 8

Unexpected Spiritual Guidance

In all of my spiritual readings I came to believe that having experiences with lack of abundance had to do with my lack of belief. I thought what I needed to do was to believe stronger in the power of God to make my financial situation different. How many of us share that same belief? The problem with lack of money is lack of belief. If we can fix the lack of belief then the "law of attraction" will bring the money. That is what I believed. That is part of the belief system built on my human foundation.

Given this belief, I began to pray every morning that God would relieve me from the financial burdens I seemed to be facing. Day after day and week after week, I received no answers to my prayers. It was almost as if there was a void in the communication between me and God. How could this be possible? I have given up everything to follow God and now I seemed disconnected. It looks like there is no avoiding economic disaster.

No Way to Avoid Economic Collapse

Finally, I received an answer to my prayers which did "not" come during my prayer time but while I was on my daily walk communing with God. The divine guidance I received was to call my attorney-friend to find out more about bankruptcy. What? Did I get that right? Am I now heading towards bankruptcy? How can this be the road to spiritual awakening? Where is this God of my understanding that is supposed to be omniscient, omnipotent, and omnipresent?

After having my "mini" breakdown, I decided to be "divinely obedient", however difficult the task at hand. I called my attorney-friend, and we talked about the "great recession of 2008" and the number of businesses that experienced financial ruin. My attorney- friend mentioned his own situation when he could not get the capital improvement loans for his multi-million dollar apartment complex. Despite all he had been through he was in an upbeat mood.

As I listened to his situation, I couldn't imagine dissolving my company which took me 20 years to build. I was moving towards economic collapse so my attorney-friend advised me to begin conserving my remaining cash to pay for essentials like mortgage, utilities and insurance.

Armed with that information, I decided it was time to let go of trying to protect my symbols of success and admit to financial failure. I had been paying out of pocket after the business closed two years prior but would never be able to repay the business debts I had accumulated. I finally got up the courage to inform all of the creditors I was moving swiftly towards "bankruptcy".

Needless to say, the creditors were not pleased, but their reactions could not begin to tell you how sick I felt in failing to meet my financial obligations. My stomach was in knots on a regular basis. I was wondering if I could hold up emotionally as this financial collapse was coming just a few short months following the death of my father. Weakly, I held on to the belief that somehow God was orchestrating this for my benefit and all would be well.

As the summer 2010 approached, the number of calls from the creditors increased with the lack of payment. I began to wonder if I had done the right thing. I had conserved my remaining cash, but it was still not going to be enough to keep me from going over the "financial cliff".

Can Things Get Any Worse

Towards the end of the summer, I got into a misunderstanding with the landlord of my office space. The landlord had informed other relatives I had not paid my office rent for the last eight months and felt I should vacate the premises. This was never formally communicated to me by the landlord but getting this information indirectly allowed me to understand why my landlord had reacted to me the way he did when I paid the most recent rent. Since he needed to receive consistent cash flow, he suggested I consider letting go of the office if I was not going to use it. I told him I would think about it.

My head was spinning with the idea of letting go of my office because my office represented my company and my company represented 20 years of my life. Upon closer reflection, I soon realized the 20 years of my life which I had spent building the company were now completely intertwined with my sense of self. For the first time, I could relate to people who were terminated from jobs after 20 or more years of service.

The loss of income is one thing, but loss of self-esteem is way beyond description. In my naïve mind, what I believed would happen when I started to follow God's guidance was I would be able to create the new business using the same foundation already in existence. To me that made all of the sense in the world because the financial systems, computer systems, branding were all in place to quickly advance any new project. However, as the scripture reminds us, "*you cannot put new wine into old wine skins*".

My new reality was starting to sink in; I was going to have to close the office. The first step in this process was to clarify the misunderstanding with the landlord. It turns out even though I was running low on money; I had never missed a rental payment for my office. In order to prove this, I went to my bank to collect copies of all checks cashed by the landlord which showed not a single payment had been missed. I presented this information to the landlord as I announced that I was moving out.

The matter was resolved but what came to light as a result of this interaction was the misunderstanding was created because of an undiagnosed level of dementia in my elderly landlord causing him to forget payments that were made. This softened my attitude towards him as a new wave of compassion filled my heart.

Be Prepared For Your Life to Fall Apart

What kind of God is this I have agreed to serve? How can my whole life falling apart be a good thing? Since I always thought serving God was a good thing, I was being challenged with my belief that "*everything works together for good for him that love the Lord*". What is God doing to my life? Is God asleep at the wheel? How can these very devastating experiences help reveal my divine self? I was so distraught that I pulled the covers back over my head and cried the deep felt sobs of profound loss.

Before I could catch myself, my sadness was replaced by anger that erupted like a volcano as I proceeded to tell God off! I told God that I did not understand why I had to go through this since I had already committed my life to God. I did not believe I had to have these kinds of human experiences because my spiritual philosophy was to protect me from such a life.

After I finished blurting out everything that was in my heart about God's lack of support for me, all I heard was a simple question. "Why are you so upset because all I am doing is taking from you those things that no longer serve you"? What??? Did I hear that correctly? That is a deep and powerful question.

As I sat straight up in my bed, I thought about all of the areas of my life that were falling apart then applied this rule of whether this activity was still serving me. I thought briefly about the romantic relationship I had which definitely was constraining me spiritually. I thought about my friends whose egos were so strong I often ended up with the short-end of the straw when dealing with them. I then thought about my consulting business which was not generating new business so it was no longer serving me.

With this new found awareness, I no longer resisted the changes in my life. As a matter of fact, I actively participated by pursing the paperwork to legally dissolve the structure of my 20 year old company with the respective state government agencies. Not only did I have to dissolve the company but now I could see the value in letting go of the rented office space.

Moving from the office was traumatic even though I was not really using the space. Still, it held a lot of emotional attachment. As the last of my furniture was moved out, I felt a tremendous sadness because I had used the office space for more than 20 years. Like my business, this space had become part of my identity. Closing the door on that office space in so many ways signified closing the door on "my past life".

I could not help but believe God would open a new door for me, however as the saying goes, "when one door closes another one opens but the hallway can be a trip"! As time went by I began to relax and see the benefits to my world falling apart. I came to understand it was necessary to dissolve the world I had created because it had become an impediment on my spiritual journey to oneness with God.

Faith in God Restored

During the fall of 2010, I was beginning to settle back into my knowingness that God was *"ordering my steps"* as I felt once again connected to my divine guidance. I knew deep in my heart I had taken all of the right steps as I closed my office, dissolved my company, and focused my attention on all things spiritual. I had not tried to find a job because I believed if I followed divine guidance the right opportunity would come to me.

In the meantime, if God wanted me to sacrifice anything, I was prepared to sell my house or sell my car. However, much of the financial pressure was taken off of me when my mother was divinely led to step forward with some financial assistance. It appears all that I had gone through during the year was now starting to strengthen me and restore my faith in God.

I remembered having a conversation about my financial situation with a friend of mine who was also a life coach. I shared with her I was learning to "truly trust" God in a new way which was good because of the financial challenge I had coming up in the next 30 days. My property taxes were due but I did not have any extra money to pay them. I remembered telling my life coaching friend that I was "not" going to worry about where the money will come from but I know God will provide. The response of my friend was "oh really? Let me know how that works out for you!" I laughed and told her I would keep her posted.

As I hung up the telephone, I remembered standing in my living room looking out the picture window into the bright sunshine with a big smile on my face. Within about one hour, the telephone rang. As I answered I could tell it was not a voice I recognized but said she had been given my telephone number as a potential consultant.

The caller wanted to know if I would be willing to do a short evaluation for a local non-profit. I agreed and with that money along with the sale of some of my gold and diamonds from my international travels, I had enough money to pay my property taxes of almost $3,000. Ladies and gentlemen, I rest my case. There really is a God who is very active in my life.

CHAPTER 9

Divine Destiny Leads
to New Start

As the holidays came and went and a New Year started, I truly believed that 2011 was going to be my year. Given all that I had been through in the past year, there was no way that I was not prepared to meet my divine destiny. As part of my daily rituals, I continued to do my prayer work, meditation and daily walks in the cold winter air seeking divine guidance from God as to what was next in my life.

Initially, there was no response from God and once again I began to get concerned. I am too far in to turn around now as I had dissolved key elements of my life destroying the bridge that led back to my old way of being. My only choice was to continue to go forward seeking the spiritual path that would allow me to live from my divine self.

This journey to spiritual awakening was proving a whole lot harder than I had imagined it would be. I believed it was going to be a simple process to implement my spiritual philosophy in my very human life. I can't believe I was so wrong. But, I was. Now what? Where do I go from here? A new year brings the hope of promises unfulfilled and this was no exception to that rule for I just knew 2011 was going to be my year.

Hijacking My Divine Destiny

By the spring of 2011, I was now singing the refrain of "oh no, here we go again" for I could not have been more disappointed with the way the year was starting out. The book sales had flat-lined, the teleclasses were unattended, and the message I received from my spirit told me to close down the new business!

What? This cannot be happening… again! I was so sure the new business was part of my divine destiny because it focused on spiritual matters. Now I am being told to shut down this new business, just like I shut down my 20 year old business. I don't understand what God wants from me! I thought I was being divinely guided when I wrote my first book and started to market it. Now I am being told this is not the direction in which I should be heading. I felt so confused and disillusioned. I needed answers and quickly!

I went into my meditation room to be able to go deeply into the silence. Due to my agitation, it took a while for me to get still enough to hear my message. When I was finally able to hear it, it went something like this:

> *"You had started on your divine destiny but then you hijacked the process by allowing your ego to determine what needed to happen. As a result, the energy you could easily access has now been denied. Divine energy cannot be misused for your personal agenda. The reason for your wanting your book to sell had everything to do with your ego trying to pretend it was 'spiritual' covering the real goal which was just to make money. Divine power is not just about making your physical life more comfortable. Divine power is about 'building the kingdom of God' by bringing change to the world structures so everyone lives from an interconnected space sharing love, peace and harmony. Once again, you misunderstand what your role is in the mosaic of humanity."*

That was a lot to take in, not the answer I had expected to hear. I was surprised at how easily my ego became a "chameleon" then sneaked into the process. Up to this point, I was unaware of my "spiritualized ego". It was quite sobering to find out I cannot do the will of God if my goal is always to keep my attention on the financial benefits to myself. For when I do that I automatically separate myself from the will of others. The journey to spiritual awakening is really about learning to dissolve my "separate self" into the oneness of God. This process which denied me the benefits of being successful with this new business was exactly what I needed for my spiritual realignment.

There was no choice; I had to disassemble all of the legal and financial structure for the new business that I created "without" divine guidance. I can't believe I have to do this again, take down the second business in just two years. To where from here? I don't know; I can't figure it out. Maybe that is what needs to happen. Maybe "I" need to stop trying to figure it out. I should just listen to what God is telling me needs to happen instead of me trying to tell God what needs to happen.

I have no idea what that is going to look like. I have no idea how to be in a space of trusting divine guidance at that level. I thought I did, but I only did from an intellectual or a philosophical level not an experiential level. I now believed I needed to learn to "walk on water". By that expression, I mean it is time for me to let go and let the rubber hit the road as I turn my spiritual philosophy into one of true "knowingness" through experience. All I needed to do was truly trust "divine guidance" by being "obedient" to the messages; then all would be well. Easier said than done…

Financial Shark Tank

By the beginning of the summer 2011, the banks had charged off the unpaid business accounts from my first business then released my financial information to a round of credit collection agencies. I had overextended my credit when I was working believing things would turn around quickly. Now like many people, I was unable to repay my business debts.

I began to weigh my options and thought about selling my house, car and declaring bankruptcy. With my credit score now so low, in effect that is what I had already done. My phone started ringing off the hook, day and night with different collection agencies calling demanding payment on business accounts. I soon started receiving threatening letters in the mail from attorneys and credit collection agencies about my lack of payment.

At first I talked to the different credit collection agencies when they called about my 20 year business that failed leaving accounts in default. Soon I found all they wanted was payment not explanations or information about other credit collection agencies calling about the same accounts. The attitudes of the collection agents I found to be offensive, as they employed their standard intimidation tactics. I had no idea where my life was going; but for now, I was caught up in the "financial shark tank".

If you have ever been in a financial shark tank, then you know the emotional toll creditors calling you can have on your self-esteem. Emotionally I was devastated by my inability to repay my debts but felt further debilitated by the way I was treated by those looking for payment.

After spending six months in the financial shark tank, I began to believe in the phrase that "money is the root of all evil". How else could a third-party be so aggressive about repayment of money that was never theirs to begin with? Meanwhile, the original party to which the business debt was owed had "charged off" the loss and received a tax write-off which is customary for "bad debts". Only in an "ego dominated" world could credit collection agencies exist as a separate industry. The development of such an industry requires one to be separate from others in order to disregard the emotional trauma their clients may be experiencing while they pursue their goal of collecting money.

As time went by, I just learned to ignore any credit collection calls in order to keep myself in a peaceful state of mind which was necessary to hear my divine guidance. I needed a new way of reacting because based on the law, these debt collection calls and letters could continue for the next five years. My attorney-friend also informed me of corruption in the credit collection business; so, even if I wanted to repay the debts at a later time, it would be hard to prove which credit collection agency truly had ownership of the accounts. Although it has been a difficult experience, I am glad to have had the financial shark tank experience. For what I came to know was that money is not the determiner of my divine destiny, God is…

Disillusioned But Not Discouraged

As the summer of 2011 progressed, my heart began to soften and my mind began to open to trusting divine guidance. With all that had happened in the last couple of months, you might think it would be the opposite: but, what actually happened was my heart and my mind became closed to my ego trying to guide my life. I always knew when my ego was involved because the benefit of what I was trying to do always accrued mostly to me.

The basis of my decision making always revolved around how I was going to financially benefit especially if what I was trying to accomplish was something good which would ultimately serve others. With this new understanding, I began to relax enjoying my summer walks and bicycle rides. I began to feel like I was becoming a different person as God blessed me with basic financial support from my mother.

In my quiet times, I no longer asked God for explanations about what was happening with my life. It seemed as if I had stopped really caring about myself in a narcissistic sort of way. I focused instead on opening my heart to blend my life into oneness with God. This is what got me up every day, this is what motivated me. What would my life look like if I stopped trying to guide it? I still wanted to know. So far the answer has been that when I stop trying to guide my life… "It fell apart"! However, I held on to the belief that into this vacuum of destruction, God would fill this space.

Divine Destiny Revealed

One day in the early fall while taking a shower the spirit of God within gave me a new message. It had been a while since I felt connected enough to receive messages. I was now given new information about a program called "ETA 2 Oneness" which would facilitate moving the world to oneness. Could this be my divine destiny? As the message continued I was told the letters "ETA" had a double meaning. ETA is associated with airports and means "estimated time of arrival". So the real question to be answered by everyone is, "What is your estimated time of arrival to oneness with God, self and others"?

The second meaning of the letters "ETA" was the spiritual life coaching process in which oneness would be taught. "E"- Embrace Your Authentic Emotionality; "T" – Trust Your Divine Guidance; and "A" – Anchor A New Way of Being. I really resonated with this concept knowing my life and my divine destiny were tied up in moving the world to oneness. This is "not" a concept I would have created in my own ego mind. This concept "ETA 2 Oneness" was truly a gift from God which came when I stopped looking for it.

This is what happens when we clean out the vessel, embrace our authentic emotionality, and trust divine guidance.

I am beginning to understand what is being required of me. It is not about what "I want", nor about what "I think", it is only about what God wills for my life. With my newfound understanding, I decided to spend more time attending church. On my first day back after summer vacation, I found myself looking at an advertisement in the church newsletter asking for teachers for the church Bible Institute. In the moment I read this information, I instantly heard a "still small voice" say, "you should teach here".

I cannot begin to tell you about the excitement that came over me in that moment, but also a level of anxiety because of my view of organized religion. Yes, I liked attending church for the rituals and gatherings of believers, but also thought of church as being parochial, closed minded and at times sanctimonious. For those reasons, this is the last place I would think God would lead me to teach.

Why would God want me to bring a spiritual life coaching program to such a traditional institution? Would this even work? When I got home from church, I found myself walking around in circles in my living room asking God, "Did I get this right"? Do you really want me to teach new spiritual life coaching concepts in a traditional institution? The answer came back a resounding "Yes"…"for you will not be the first for Jesus brought a new philosophy to the Jewish people". With that answer, all I could do was laugh.

The following day I called the Dean of the Bible Institute and told her of my spiritual experience in church the day before. I told her I was being guided by God to offer a new type of spiritual teaching. She told me to attend the meeting of the new instructors the next day so we could further discuss what program I was to bring forward. The meeting went well and I decided to start by teaching a series of spiritual life coaching seminars based on the process given to me in "ETA 2 Oneness".

To my surprise, my churchgoing members were very open to this new understanding finding the discussions useful. The main theme of the seminars was focused on why it is so difficult to live our spiritual beliefs in the "real world". Spiritual life coaching concepts shared were easily embraced by those in attendance. Word spread about this new type of training and others participated in future seminars.

A year had passed and I found I had taught seven seminars. At the closing awards ceremony for the church Bible Institute, I also found out I had the largest number of people to participate in my trainings. In my heart, I knew that being in this situation was truly a blessing from God and the result of trusting divine guidance. You know when you're in the right place in terms of your divine destiny when what brings you joy is something you love to do. Living from this place never feels like work.

During the beginning of 2012, I turned my full attention to creating the foundation for a third business in as many years. One day I was guided to create the website for ETA 2 Oneness using the template I had used with my last business. As had become my ritual, I would do prayers before I touched anything related to ETA 2 Oneness. The reason I did this is because I know in my heart that I did not create the concept ETA 2 Oneness, therefore I have no idea where it is supposed to go. There is no way to create without a consistent connection with God. The website came pretty quickly as a result of my following divine guidance.

About a week later, I was guided to build the foundation for "social media" including setting up new accounts on Facebook, Twitter, and YouTube. I was divinely guided to use the same name "ETA 2 Oneness" across all social media platforms. The idea of being able to use the same name across all platforms is virtually impossible these days because all social media sites have "hundreds of millions" of global customers. Trying to find a unique name that is not already in use is virtually impossible for one site, much less three sites. So you can imagine the big smile on my face by the end of the day when I realized that I was successful in securing all three social media sites with the same name. In that moment I knew God was truly in the midst of it all.

I began to feel that I was on my path to fulfilling my divine destiny, but also knew from the last business that I could "not" run ahead of God. It was only my job to wait and become spiritually obedient to God. Because of the seminars I had conducted and the results experienced by people who attended my trainings, I came to believe this combination of spiritual philosophy and life coaching was very effective. I knew in time I would be released to reach a lot more people.

What I learned on my spiritual journey so far is that in order to move towards oneness with God, you must be *"willing to give up everything and follow me"* as Jesus told his disciples. My life now bears no resemblance to the life I had before. What I thought would happen in this transition from my human self to my divine self was it would be effortless, like being on one side of the mountain and needing to get around to the other side.

In my naïve mind I thought it would be as simple as going around the top of the mountain, when in actuality what was required was for me to descend the mountain altogether and come back up the other side. For those whose lives have already fallen apart, just know you are deep into your spiritual journey; so, continue to trust divine guidance for "the only way out is through", with no sure guide but God.

CHAPTER 10

Another Roller Coaster Ride

When I decided to truly give my life to God and get on purpose, the God I met was not a "Santa Claus God". By this I mean God was not here to fulfill my heart's desires with an endless stream of things resulting in acquisitions and accumulation. My belief system about how God functioned was based on my human conditioning. Therefore, I had false conceptions about who God was. In my mind, if I am "good" then God would give me everything I asked for. But I found this not to be true as I started to truly trust God.

As you can see from what I have shared so far, the first thing that happened was I was forced to alter my human values by the loss of many things "I valued". Up to March of 2009, my trust in God was truly an "intellectual exercise" not a "tangible experience" of the presence of God. For you see to have a tangible experience of God requires one to consciously step out on "faith" following the divine impulses often resulting in uncertainty. It is in the uncertainty of life where your faith in God can be tested and thereby strengthened.

One of the challenges for those of us on the spiritual path is the ability to truly trust God. How do you know if you are making spiritual progress in trusting God? When you are wrestling with your faith, being emotionally authentic with God, and even "hating on God", then know you are truly making progress on your spiritual path. Many of us think we trust God as we pray to God for the desires of our hearts for ourselves or for others.

My question of the moment, "Is praying to God the same thing as trusting God"? I have prayed to God and been upset when God did not deliver what I thought I deserved. What I found interesting as I moved more into my spiritual awakening is that my concept of God was truly limited. I didn't realize how much I wanted God to fit my understanding as a "Santa Claus God" that delivered my heart desires because I was a "good person" trying to do the right thing. My prayers to God were things I believed would create a better life for me and others.

Never did I stop to think that the desires of my heart were created out of my human conditioning which allowed for my ego to navigate my reality. In this way, I was the determiner of what was "good" and what was "bad". It never dawned on me to challenge my moral beliefs that came with this duality. As far as I was concerned, if I decided something was good or bad, then the truth of the matter is that it was good or bad. Often the morals of society supported my belief which reinforced my own judgment.

How can we get from the place where our human judgment of what is good or bad is no longer the compass by which we guide our lives? The reason I am asking this question is because what is good or bad is very much dependent upon how you see reality. The way you see reality is totally dependent on your own experiences and your own enculturation. Therefore the prayers you send up to God are those things which fit into your reality that you feel God can help you with. Do we truly trust God? Or are we looking for a "Santa Claus God" to just give us our hearts desires?

Too many of us do not know what it really means to "trust God" for we tend to trust God only as long as God's will is joined with our personal agenda. As long as we hold this belief that God is here to service us and not us being here to service God, then all of us on a spiritual path are destined for failure.

To truly trust God, we must allow our personal agenda to be subservient to God's will. We need to let go of our resistance and belief that if we completely trust God somehow we will be punished or not provided for. We must also understand trusting God does not mean abdicating responsibility for ourselves. One of the important things in all decisions that come from God is the outcome should benefit everyone. This means you too must be the beneficiary of all divine decisions.

Your life is not initially made easier because you decide to follow God. Quite the opposite, because you need to absorb a new value system you need to change tracks from your human belief system to your divine belief system. Initially it seems in many ways your life becomes much more difficult. I was not prepared for this new reality for I had believed that to trust in God meant God would provide for my every desire as long as I was in spiritual alignment.

What is spiritual alignment without trust in God's guidance? Many of us on the spiritual path believe that spiritual alignment comes in the form of studying the Bible, reciting affirmations, meditating in the proper positions, attending church services, or upholding moral standards. However to trust in God's guidance we must loosen our grip on the cultural rituals which are the tools which point the way to God, but of themselves are not God.

We must come to understand that our ego cannot guide our decision-making and dictate the terms of our spiritual alignment. It is our persistence in the pursuit of spiritual alignment that allows God to enter into the process and take control of our divine destiny. This often means things we value from a human perspective may be lost. In my false bravado, I was more than willing to detach myself from all of the stuff or "tan-phys" (tangible physical reality) that holds humans in the grasp of their egos.

From the moment I decided to find out "what happens to my life if I don't guide it", the next five years proved to me that I did not know who God truly was. During this time, all of the things I agreed to put on the altar for God were taken-- my business, my career, my financial credibility, my house, my car, my friendships, and my health. All of these things defined me as an individual and reinforced my perception of myself as successful in society.

What happens to your sense of self when those things you value no longer define you? For me it became a slippery slope into a world of depression for I no longer felt I had value. How do you operate every day when nothing in your world is important or necessary? How can this level of detachment be a good thing? Where is God in all of this loss? How can this type of life be the will of God?

As I struggled through my trust issues with God, there were times when I understood the need to separate me from the material world that defined me. There were other times I did not understand why I was left so isolated and alone. I would often talk to God in an angry tone because I believed my desire was good to be in the oneness with God. If that was my desire, then why was everything I valued being taken away from me? It did not take long for me to see how attached I was to those things in life that were brought to me for my comfort. There was no separation between me and my things therefore there was no room for God to operate in my world. For how can God operate in a world where the focus is on acquisition and accumulation?

This was a really hard lesson for me to learn that God was not punishing me by separating me from the things I valued. God was actually teaching me to trust by showing me the unreality of relying so heavily on stuff. I had gotten to the point where all my stuff and the pursuit of stuff got in the way of human relationships. Somehow we get so focused on what our individual needs and wants are that we bypass the ability to truly just love and support one another. In this chapter, I will continue with my life lessons as I share my struggles in learning to trust God.

The Christmas that Passed Me By

Throughout the year, many of us count the months until the Christmas holidays. If you are like me you can truly feel a difference in people during this time of the year. It seems as if we are "one big happy family" all around the globe. People display random acts of kindness as well as allow little slights to go unpunished. It is this time of the year that people tend to be more giving, more open, more concerned with others besides themselves.

I love the Christmas holidays for this is truly a time that it feels like I live in utopia with the medium of exchange being "love". How much love can you give? How much love are you open to receiving? With this being my favorite holiday, you can imagine my dismay at the idea of "Christmas passing me by".

During the year of 2013, I was blessed by God to work on a short term consulting project in New Orleans. The project went well and we were at the end of the project as we approached the Christmas holidays. Unfortunately for me the arrival of my final payment came too late for me to participate in all of the holiday gift-giving. What made this particularly interesting was that the week before I had slipped on the ice, fallen down the stairs, and was now home on crutches as a way to allow my ankle to heal.

What kind of God is this that would take me on another roller coaster ride? I was speeding into the Christmas holidays with so many challenges: on crutches with a hospital bill of almost $3,000, no ability to pay bills, heating oil tank almost empty, relatives involved in a family feud over denial of Alzheimer's, no clients for new business, no money to publish this book you are reading, and no significant other to share this stress with. This seemed to be a recipe for disaster. The money I was anticipating came too late... too late to shop for Christmas... too late to pay bills on time... too late for me to value the "almighty dollar" as power to make my life different.

My mind drifted back to the slang word "bread" which was equated with "money". Something happened that I could not explain, but my reality shifted and my energy soared as I truly began to understand the meaning of "*man does not live by bread alone".* In my Christmas that was passing me by, I gained the most valuable insight. I realized I could never be in a place where "God is not" for God is omnipresent. Experiencing this concept allowed me to survive the apparent lack.

It was during one of the most difficult holiday seasons of my life that I began to feel gratitude and appreciation for what God had done in my life, not for what was wrong in the current moment. I began to see I took a lot of things for granted never saying "thank you" to God for any of the blessings I experienced.

I began to realize there was no way to trust a God I could not feel gratitude and appreciation for. My limited perception of who and what God was in the past depended on what God did for me. As I started the New Year of 2014, I was now mindful of how I could be of service to God because I was no longer connected to the tangible physical reality in such a way that it required God to service me.

What do you Mean No Oil?

It is easy to sing God's praises when things are going well, but when you don't get an answer to a prayer you have requested, it becomes more difficult to be in the oneness with God. How can we be in the oneness with God when we don't feel like God is in the oneness with us? Sometimes we have to understand that what God is doing is stretching us beyond our human capacity and opening us up to a divine way of being.

To get from our humanness to our divinity requires us to move through some difficult times while being authentic in our emotional expression and wrestling with our faith. That lesson seemed to continue during the winter of 2014 in the city of Philadelphia. It was at that time the city experienced the second highest snowfall totals in recorded in the history. For any number of reasons, this will be the winter I will always remember. I will remember being one of many moving around on crutches because of a fall on the ice. I will also remember the callousness of those in business. This is that story.

During this snowy winter in the Philadelphia area, the average temperature was almost 20 degrees below normal causing me to burn heating oil at an alarming rate. By the end of February of 2014, I had already spent close to $3,000 to heat my house over the last five months which was way beyond the yearly budget. I knew I would be getting financial help from my family in the coming month while I waited for my house to be sold. What I was not prepared for was requesting oil from my energy company and having them say "No"!

What do you mean no oil delivery as the gauge on my oil tank reached "empty" and the temperatures outside hovered in the single digits? In these types of temperatures, most people know the importance of heat goes way beyond just staying warm because without heat your pipes can burst causing even bigger problems.

I could not wrap my brain around how an oil company could be so callous in its refusal to deliver additional oil to a long standing customer going through a difficult time? Well, first I must acknowledge my "contribution to the chaos" because I was definitely at fault when I could not afford to keep up with the payments of oil that were previously delivered. Normally, I would have been on a budget plan, but because I had "not" anticipated the sale of the house falling through in 2013, which left me stuck in the house through the winter being forced to pay out of pocket for each delivery.

I understand the need of companies to maintain financial integrity with regards to their business dealings, but this was no ordinary winter and I was no ordinary customer. I had been a customer with this company for more than 10 years. In that time, I had paid them approximately $40,000 for providing services and oil delivery. At the moment I needed them most, they refused to give me even one drop of oil unless I paid them the total outstanding balance of $775 plus another $600 to provide the minimum amount of oil they would deliver to me.

How could an energy company put profits ahead of human compassion? How could the workers go to sleep at night knowing they denied oil to a long-standing customer who was experiencing hard times? It was in this moment I realized how misguided our ego thought system had become and how insensitive we have made ourselves to the suffering of others.

As I sat there in my cold house with 10 inches of snow outside and more on the way, at first I was angry. But as time passed my anger turned to sadness as I thought about how I lived in a society where the only goal of success was pursuit of the "almighty dollar". We have lost our humanity as we give no thought to the consequences of our behavior on others. In that moment I realized, we need business people to be on a spiritual path, who can make decisions that benefit not only their "bottom line" but the whole of humanity.

In getting quiet, I began to communicate with my spirit which guided me to contact another oil company which took credit cards and delivered smaller amounts of oil. As the winter gave way to spring and oil was no longer needed, I felt blessed and thank God for having survived such a difficult winter.

God's Guidance Sometimes Makes No Sense

We think as spiritual beings we would come to understand God's guidance but there are times when we get messages from the "still small voice" directing us to do something that sometimes just makes no sense. We have to get to a place where we simply trust God with our only response being "obedience". We have to know beyond a shadow of a doubt that God's guidance will ultimately prove to be the best solution to any situation.

What happens to most of us is because there is no external proof that the internal guidance is a good one, our ego begins to alter the outcome by injecting new decisions into the process. This will not allow for the universe to conspire to support us because we have now taken control of what we believe is a better outcome for ourselves. Only when we have had enough experiences to show us that the internal guidance from God is far superior to our ego guidance then we begin to be obedient to God without resistance.

It is a process to get to this place on our journey of spiritual awakening. However, once you are there and you receive messages that have no external verification, you do not hesitate to be obedient to divine guidance. You know the reason for God's decision will soon be revealed if you just stay the course… "watch and wait". Let me give you an example of what I am talking about.

After the "Christmas that passed me by", everything I had been through allowed me to understand the command of Jesus who said to his disciples, *"give up everything and follow me"*. I now realized this request was "not" symbolic because at this point in my life I had given up everything which included: my business, my career, my friendships, and my car. The only material possession I had left was my house and now I was being asked to let go of that as well.

Before I got deeply into my journey of spiritual awakening, if anybody had said to me that following God would mean that I would "lose everything I valued", I would've told them they were crazy. But as I look to put my house on the market, I reviewed the experiences of the last few years only to realize God's ways are truly not man's ways. It took me a minute to understand the more I let go of my tangible physical reality, the less stress I felt and the more secure my relationship became with God.

As the New Year of 2014 started, I heard the still small voice tell me "not" to put my house on the market until the week of January 20th. I did not ask "why", I was simply obedient. As I shared this message with a member of my family, I was challenged to go around the message that I heard. My response at this point on my spiritual journey was that I could not go around this message because it was "given for a reason" even though at that time I did not know what the reason was.

When your trust in God is so complete, your only response is obedience and a total lack of resistance. I was most curious to watch for the revealing of the reason why I was given this message in the first place. As the first week past uneventful, I stood very watchful as I entered the second week of January. It was during the end of the second week of January that the divine guidance I had been given was made plain.

My initial real estate agent from 2013, was also a relative, but was now caught on the "wrong" side of the family feud. Although we still got along great, it was very awkward to continue to use her as my real estate agent. I was on my way home one night when I heard the message to "release her" from being my real estate agent and to find a new company. That message was shared with my family member who was my agent and she totally understood. Since this process of finding a new agent took several days, by the time everything was settled, it was now the week of January 20th!

I shared this story mainly because we have to get to the point when we are given divine guidance to simply trust it instead of looking for external verification of the message or deviating from our sense of obligation simply because of our human uncertainty. If we can hold on, "all things are revealed in time" and the path we take under God's guidance will always be the best path to the desired outcome.

Shaken and Stirred

Now that my house was on the market, I looked forward to getting out from under the financial stress of managing a house. I believed that selling my house was also the last step in my willingness to "give up everything" to follow God. I was way beyond the point of spiritual philosophy in making this final decision to sell my house. I was operating under divine guidance; so I believed selling my house would be a fairly simple and quick process.

Sometimes when you are coming to the end of some situation, you are shaken and stirred in a way that is unexpected. It turns out I was right about the house selling fairly quickly, but I was wrong about the sale being fairly simple. The house sold in just 40 days despite the weekly snowstorms in February. People were coming to see my house before the snowstorms and after the snowstorms which kept me busy making sure the walkways were shoveled.

I was trusting God that this was the right time to put the house on the market for sale, but what I was not prepared for was the additional cost associated with selling the house. As my limited finances were dwindling because I continued to spend an unusual amount of money in heating oil, I was left with very little money to fix anything but I continued on with the process for selling the house.

There was an "open house" scheduled within a few weeks of getting a new real estate agent which would allow people to view the house as they considered the option to buy it. The day before the open house, I was in the basement doing laundry when I noticed there was water leaking around the hot water heater. I immediately called my contractor who came by to inspect. He concluded the hot water tank was defective and in need of replacement.

Oh my God, how can my hot water tank be busted the day before my "open house"!

How am I supposed to replace a hot water tank when it will cost me more money than I have left in my bank account? I took a moment to have a conversation with God and in that time was given guidance as to how to solve my problem. In short, I ordered the hot water tank online with major appliance store where I could pay for it with credit and my contractor could pick it up. Unfortunately, I was still left with the installation charges which were not cheap but manageable. Disaster avoided, "open house" successful.

My real estate agent decided to continue to be aggressive in pushing the sale of the house, so she scheduled a second "open house" a couple of weeks later. Although there was no snow anticipated before this open house, there was a blast of arctic air that sent temperatures plunging into the negative numbers. This left my basement feeling extremely cold so I decided to borrow some space heaters to warm it up for the visitors who would be inspecting the house. When I got the space heaters home, I plugged them in and turned them on "high" to heat the basement quickly.

In the meantime, I went upstairs to take care of some other errands before returning in about an hour to turn down the space heaters. To my dismay, the space heaters were "not" working and upon further inspection I found the outlets that the space heaters had been plugged into were all blown out. Once again this is happening the day before an open house.

My first concern was with the space heaters, hoping they were not damaged because they did not belong to me. I gathered them together, put them in my car, and ran them back to the office where I picked them up. When I got there, I immediately plugged them in to be sure they were both working. To my great relief, there was no damage to either one of the space heaters.

The next day the open house went on as planned but I knew once there was a bid on the house that I would have to make arrangements to repair the electrical outlets. The following day, upon awakening I heard my spirit tell me the solution to my problem. So I jumped up, ran to the basement, and began resetting the electrical box. To my surprise, the power was restored to the electrical outlets. My fear of damage being done was over and another disaster averted.

Shortly after the second open house, there was a bid put in and accepted on the house. Finally, there would be a new owner. In anticipation of the house inspection, I began the repair of small things such as the downspouts, gutters, sidewalks, and steps. Since I had a house inspection the year before when the house was on the market, I knew the new house inspection would not find anything of serious consequence to be repaired. I was content in making sure that these obvious things were taken care of.

I was in a pretty good mood looking out the window in my kitchen to my beautiful backyard while marveling at the strength of the wind. I felt secure because I was inside of my house. I thought to myself I was glad I did not wait until the last minute to take care of the small things on the exterior of the house since the inspection was rapidly approaching. All of a sudden, I heard a loud boom and a continuous banging sound. I opened the back door and found the storm door had been taken by the wind and was lodged between the beams of the patio.

As I tried to pull the storm door closed, I found I could not get it back under the beam to pull it shut. As the storm door kept banging in the 40 to 50 mph winds, I closed the main door and fell to my knees asking God, "What do you want from me?…How am I now supposed to fix this new problem"?

I truly felt "shaken and stirred" by all of the recent unexpected repairs with so little money to handle anything. I was truly "living on the edge" financially and did not have extra money to replace a storm door. In that moment, a sense of calm came over me as I released the problem to God. I got up off of my knees and went back to doing dishes while the storm door continued to bang in the wind.

A few minutes later while standing at the kitchen window, I saw in the distance one of my neighbors who often did repair work for me. I ran through the house and out the front door to get his attention. As the wind started to calm down, he came to the back of the house and looked at the storm door. He remarked about the strength of the wind gust to force the door up under the patio beam. In addition, the force of the wind loosened the glass panes in the door and caused a small split in the top of the door.

My neighbor used all of his strength to pull the door back under the beam so that it would close correctly. Now the issue was how to repair the frame of the door so the glass panes would not fall out. I ended up running him to the hardware store where we purchased the required materials. It took him about a half an hour to repair the door.

The good news for me was the incident was over, the door was almost as good as new and the total cost of repairs was $20. As I bolted the storm door closed, I just smiled and thought nothing is impossible with God if we live from this "new way of being".

PART 3

Anchor A New Way of Being

CHAPTER 11

God's Will is Really Better

No matter what you think, it is virtually impossible to have a "comprehensive view" of reality being that you are only one person in a world of 7 billion people. That in and of itself should give you room to pause whenever you are tempted to say your answer to something is the "only way" or the "right way".

In addition to a limited view of reality, most of us don't understand how proposed goals or desired outcomes are filtered through our "spiritualized ego" thereby creating distortions. Given this perspective, how can you know for sure how your skills and talents should be used for the benefit of humanity and in the building of God's kingdom on earth?

Practices often promoted as essential to your spiritual growth include: visioning processes, setting intentions, taking action steps, memorizing scripture and reciting daily affirmations. All of these practices work to provide you with the life you are seeking to manifest.

What is not talked about by those on the spiritual path is that this "current way of being" is limited. Whatever goals you set, whatever outcomes you seek are all ego-driven because you are the one creating them from your limited slice of reality. There is really only one true desire we can carry as humans which will help to reveal the "divine self". That is a heartfelt desire to be in "oneness with God".

Aligning with God's Will

I have only caught glimpses of how this can work because of my willingness to detach myself from everything I thought would bring me joy. I have allowed myself to be put into situations where I could not control the outcome. By taking great risks to follow divine guidance, it allowed me to "feel" God's presence while providing outcomes I never would have dreamt possible. We have all heard it said, but few of us have really tested the belief "God's will for your life is really better than your own personal will".

Now is the time to test this theory by aligning yourself with the will of God and letting go of your personal agenda. Many may not believe, but our decision making abilities based upon our five senses is truly limited. Only when tuning to a multi-sensory level and accessing "something told me" can we benefit from divine guidance which is far superior to our human decision making ability.

Our human way of making decisions involves analyzing tangible data then arriving at some conclusion in order to take appropriate action. This "old way of being" is very limiting because we do not take into account any information that does not fit into our current "frame of reference". As humans, according to a concept in the book "A Course in Miracles", we have a tendency to separate segments of reality by the changeable scales of desire. By this I mean if you desire something, you will always allow for it...but when you no longer desire it, you will then judge against it.

This "new way of being" does not require you to use your analytical skills in any form or fashion in determining your reality. Your new way of being is now based upon your oneness with God. It is from this place of being obedient to divine guidance that you now make decisions which already account for all variables ensuring the outcomes are optimal.

How do we move towards a new way of being, allowing God's will to reign supreme? Awareness is the key to change. If we just realize there is a new way of being available to us, then we can begin the shift. Part of what keeps us stuck in our limited human perspective is the benefit or payoff that come to us from being "master of the universe" in our own world. We too often see ourselves as "demi- gods" literally operating on the belief that "everything is under our dominion".

Unfortunately, we are using our limited human self to control our external reality to manifest the outcomes we desire. This way of being results in conflict and chaos because most of us are making decisions and taking actions without first releasing our own emotional baggage. Therefore those decisions are made with a "closed heart", not considering the impact of our decisions on others. We may give "lip service" to the concept of supporting and including others in our decisions, but in reality our actions don't follow.

We have to learn to open our hearts by embracing our authentic emotionality. There is no way around this. There are no shortcuts. You cannot operate under God's will without seeking to be one with yourself first, then with others. Many of us believe we can skip this step of going into the painful memories of our past. Instead by simply attending church, reading our Bibles or praying daily, somehow the anger and hatred lodged deep in our hearts towards others will somehow disappear. It is well known in scripture that if you have offended any man, then "*leave your gifts at the altar and go reconcile with him*" before returning to honor God.

One of the reasons for reconciliation is that anger and hatred in your heart continues to create a separation from others. Separation is not the road to oneness. There are no exceptions to this rule. All of us must look within ourselves to find those dark places, those painful places, those secret places where we are projecting anger and criticism onto others because we cannot be one with ourselves. We must look for our own "shadow beliefs".

Own Your Contribution to the Chaos

It is time to create a new way of being in which we take full responsibility for who we are and what we have created in our lives. Many of us will admit the fact that negative consequences have resulted from our bad decisions. The good news is the past is really now in the past. It is time to let go and get beyond the triggers that throw us into past memories. How do we do that? One of the first things you can do is look at your current life and recall situations where you feel "triggered". As you embrace your authentic emotionality, you will uncover the patterns in your life that need to be healed.

For many of us who have become victims of someone's bad behavior, it is not very easy to get beyond what they have done to us. But, the deeper you dig within the scenario or the situation that occurred, the more you will find you were not totally blameless. I said before "anger is a projected emotion". If we do not deal with our "contribution to the chaos" we continue to focus our anger on what someone else did to us instead of what we have contributed to the situation. We must take personal responsibility for every decision and every situation in which we find ourselves, for this is part of the new way of being.

The road to oneness is very difficult because you are not allowed to blame anyone for anything that happens in your life. As you begin to deal with the painful or hurtful memories, you bring to the surface unexpressed emotionality. It is this feeling of being heard that we are all seeking. We all have an inherent desire to be treated with love and kindness and when that does not happen, there needs to be an outlet for the feelings of anger and resentment arising within us. As you continue to release the bottled up feelings, what starts to happen is you become much less reactionary or triggered by the bad behavior of others. From this place of peace and calm, you can stay connected to your divine guidance.

Connecting to Your Divine Self

There is no way for you to take yourself to this "new way of being" because the ego's job is one of control and dominance… not subservience. In this new way of being the power of God begins to come through you, but not for your personal use. This idea is alien to your ego which sees everything in its path as something for its individual pleasure. This inability to see beyond one's individual needs to see the needs of the collective is what limits the ego's viability. Therefore, unless you are anchored to your divine self, your ego will try to misuse the power of God to its advantage to hurt or harm others.

The most frequently asked questions are: "If I connect to my divine self, does it mean that I no longer have feelings, emotions, desires, wants or needs? Do I have to sacrifice my way of being in order to be one with God"? In many ways the answer to both questions is "yes". The way you live your life will change and you will initially see this as a "sacrifice" because as your values change, you probably will have to let go of some of the things you believed brought you peace, happiness, and prosperity.

Once again, as was previously stated, since "nothing that we see means anything"; your ego's standards for peace, happiness, and prosperity will have to be replaced by God's view of reality. The process of transcendence from our human self to our divine self is what allows us to become a "clear channel for God's use".

CHAPTER 12

No Longer a Separate Self

What is the "great spiritual awakening" that I am talking about? What does that really mean? The great spiritual awakening is the place we arrive at individually and collectively, when we no longer see the needs and desires of others as separate from our own. What makes the spiritual awakening unique is that the ability to feel connected to others is not forced, nor controlled by disciplining your thoughts with "sugary insincerity". This way of seeing reality is habitual and natural as you begin to see everyone as an extension of yourself.

Right now many of us can think about the need and desires of others; but, we do not think about them on the same level in which we think about our own needs. Far too many of us speak about the concerns of others, but our actions are non-existent or insufficient. In the spiritual awakening there will be no such thing as a "separate self".

You cannot make decisions that benefit only you and be okay with that, as we do in our current reality. In the future, as the spiritual awakening takes root, the inclination to make decisions that only benefit you will no longer even cross your mind because that way of being will "not" bring you happiness.

Many of us are prepared for the spiritual awakening because of our study of spiritual philosophy; but, if you are not connected to a church, temple, mosque, center or a community of believers, then your ability to anchor yourself in this new way of being will be challenged. A community of like-minded people allows one protection, as we each struggle to bring forth our divine self without the fear of judgment from others.

There is more compassion, understanding, acceptance and tolerance built into communities of believers. Because the divine law has already been taught in these places, the challenge for us is to move ourselves into alignment by dealing with our emotional baggage. Once we release our emotional baggage, then we can open ourselves up to becoming a "clear channel for God's use".

Clear Channel for God's Use

What is a "clear channel for God's use"? Answer… it is someone who dedicates their life to God 24 hours a day/7 days a week, allowing themselves to be "divinely obedient" to the will of God, in order to anchor God's kingdom on earth. This person stays in constant contact with the spirit of God within while going about their daily tasks. In every situation in which they find themselves, they are open to divine impulses that will guide them to make decisions which always benefit the whole of which they are a part. I have worked hard on becoming a clear channel for God's use and as a result there are times when I am guided to do things that initially make no sense. Let me give you an example.

I was looking out of my home office window while dictating sections of this book when I was guided to stop working. I sat still for a few moments focusing my attention on the man across the street clearing the yard of leaves and branches. The newly painted exterior of the house was a peaceful tan color with white trim. As I continued to watch the worker blow leaves into a pile in the center of the yard, I noticed that he was starting to move around the yard picking up small branches. What caught my attention was he was putting the branches into a big black plastic bag. It was in that moment I had a divine impulse, so I headed for my basement.

I live in a very environmentally conscious community with strict regulations about recycling. I knew our trash collectors would "not" pick up the black plastic bags of branches because they were not in the proper designated paper lawn bags. I saw the worker had used four of such lawn bags already but had run out. My spirit guided me to my basement to pick up more lawn bags to take across the street to the worker. As I approached holding out more of the designated lawn bags, he confirmed he had run out of them leaving only a large box of plastic trash bags.

I gave him the extra lawn bags as I explained the recycling process in our community which collects lawn bags each fall to create mulch. In the springtime, trucks dump the mulch onto selected parking lots around the township so residents can have a source of soil for gardening activities. He understood and used the bags I provided to pick up the remaining branches. As I walked back across the street, I smiled to myself saying this is what living in "oneness" is really all about.

In this new way of being, we don't wait for someone to make a mistake then criticize them or shame them for not "doing the right thing". We are quickly moved to offer our assistance; not based upon our arrogant interpretation of what needs to happen, but based upon the divine impulses. Given that clear channels are divinely obedient, we can move into action immediately, without questioning or analyzing what we are being guided to do for another, knowing the result will benefit everyone.

In walking back to my house, I gave no thought that somehow I would be at a disadvantage because I shared some of my lawn bags with this worker. The interesting thing I found out about using divine guidance is that I have never been guided to do things that are detrimental to me.

All solutions are a "win-win" keeping in place, harmony and balance. Hopefully we will soon learn that "oneness is a blessing that benefits all".

One Global Community

Seeing ourselves as one global community connected to each other is not new to any of us. Most of us "wear our hearts on our sleeves" when we look at how the world rallies around communities impacted by natural disasters such as hurricanes or earthquakes. The generosity of spirit is always on display during such times because it is our natural inclination due to our connectedness with one another. This human bond that we all share is not something that is easily broken; but, it is something we don't always keep in the forefront of our minds.

It is only in the moments when we are operating out of our separateness that we are capable of hurting one another, with our displays of bad behavior. This way of being, of seeing yourself as "separate from others" is an idea that must give way to the "oneness of humanity". There is no way to separate from others and continue to live in a global community. What happens to one happens to all, because our interconnectedness is like an ocean wave that starts in one place and touches shores far away.

All of us can see the movement of oneness that is spreading across our planet as "corporate responsibility" is blossoming, causing millionaires and billionaires to get involved in causes to help those less fortunate. It is no longer unique to see lots of money raised by celebrities for a "good cause". As a matter of fact, it is becoming the norm for them to share their financial blessings. As some of us experience economic challenges, it is good to see people in our global community willing to share. The clearer you become, the more conscious you become in serving our global community in some capacity.

Releasing Our Judgmental-Self

The path to spiritual awakening is not by way of trying to control your external environment, but more so by unscrambling your internal environment. For your external environment is only a reflection of your internal beliefs, thoughts and behaviors. If you want to make a change to your external environment, you need to shift your internal thinking. The major shift required is to those beliefs and behaviors that keep you anchored to a separate self, reflected in phrases such as: "I am right about this" or "I don't care what happens to them". These types of phrases show your commitment to your ego.

Anything in your belief system that causes you to judge others is there for a reason. You must become aware of the root cause of why you feel the need to judge. In short, judgment according to spiritual life coaching is a direct result of a "shadow belief" of needing to feel superior to others because of a deep seeded belief in your own inferiority. Ironically, the behavior exhibited is the exact opposite of what the person may be trying to project.

Understanding this concept is one of the reasons as a spiritual life coach I tend to laugh at people who appear to be judgmental, arrogant, or belligerent because I know internally they are weak and insecure. One of the reasons we judge is keep the attention off of our own shortcomings. It is easy to judge something you have never experienced; but, once you have dealt with a situation, you will not be so quick to judge others going through a similar situation.

If we look deeper into the concept of judgment, we will see judgment is interconnected with our other lower level vibrations such as fear, anger, frustration, hatred, powerlessness, hopelessness, and helplessness. These lower level vibrations are what we fight against wanting to experience. From a human perspective, these emotions are inevitable, but from a divine perspective, these lower level emotions are unnecessary because they are the by-product of seeing the needs of another as unrelated to your own. As long as you allow your ego to be your guide and pursue only your own goals and desires then consider these lower level vibrations to be your companions.

You cannot be critical and judgmental of another based upon your own distorted view of reality and expect to enter into the oneness with God. We must enter into the "arc of peace" two by two taking always into account the needs of our brothers and sisters. For no one reaches oneness alone with fear dominating their hearts instead of love.

To end the sleep walking, we must make our primary desire to be in the oneness with God by being in the oneness with each other. It is God who will direct your path if you allow your mind to become an "instrument of divine attunement" instead of the "vehicle for personal creativity". In this way, you become a clear channel for God's use and life becomes a beautiful journey.

Anger As A Tool To Force Compliance

In addition to judgment, another thing that keeps us anchored in our human way of being is our easy use of anger and violence. We give no thought to others as we project onto them our anger and rage. If forethought was given to the impact of your words, your intonations, or the hostility on your face, you would not subject another person to your anger. As has been mentioned before "anger" is a projected emotion which comes from deep within a person. For rarely is there anything in the external environment that requires anyone to be that upset with somebody to exhibit that level of intensity of anger.

The assumption is often made that people are doing things on purpose to anger you. That is not true. Often, people are so caught up in their separateness that you are not even a thought in their mind, which is why a decision they make can have a negative impact on you. Sometimes it is your emotional reaction of anger which triggers the anger in another. In my spiritual life coaching, I found anger is often used to conceal hurt, pain, or sadness. The real thing that needs to be dealt with is the emotion buried deep within us. We have gotten to a place in society where we allow anger, violence, and hostility to be more acceptable human emotions than hurt, pain or sadness.

Our human perspective makes it unacceptable to show weakness because we believe we can be easily taken advantage of; but, operating from our divine self, the fear of anyone wielding power over us disappears. How can this be the case? The ability of someone to wield power over you is directly proportional to your understanding of your "inherent invulnerability". As we move towards our divine self, we come to a place where we realize anything anyone has ever done to us has never altered the "essential essence" of who God created us to be.

For example, victims of sexual or physical assault could continue to be troubled by their experiences believing someone caused them pain or hurt; but, in truth the pain or hurt was only to their physical bodies. Therefore at a soul level, no one can alter the "essential essence" of who God created you to be. For you are not merely "material" but you are "Spirit", rendering you "inherently invulnerable" to alteration by human hands.

Many of us have so identified with our bodies and our possessions we think of these things as us. Things are not you. Seeing ourselves as bodies or possessions forces us to spend our time in constant conflict, trying to protect what we think of as our identity. During the process of spiritual awakening, more of us will learn to separate the essential essence of ourselves from the events in our lives, for it is this process that gives space for the divine self to emerge.

CHAPTER 13

Going Deeper With Forgiveness

L et's talk about the role of forgiveness in this new way of being. The reason true forgiveness is necessary is because it opens the way for oneness, making us aware of our conscious interconnection with one another. This allows our divine self to emerge spreading pure love to everyone who crosses our path because we no longer project painful memories into present circumstances.

If we have "not" truly forgiven, then the capacity of our hearts to share love is limited in proportion to the amount of forgiveness we withhold from others. It is difficult to see the amount of work that really needs to be done on this issue because most of us are hiding behind the veil of "forgiveness lite".

Forgiveness Offered Too Soon

If asked about difficult relationships in our lives, most will say they have forgiven those people. Have you forgiven your mother? Absolutely! Have you forgiven your father? Truly, I have! Have you forgiven your ex-husband? No problem, we are still friends… I would beg to differ with most people who say they have "forgiven" someone with whom they had a difficult relationship, because the offer of forgiveness usually comes "too soon" in the healing process.

When we are hurt or when we are in pain, we are in no condition to forgive anybody for anything. The first step in truly learning to forgive is the full self-expression of the pain that is in our own hearts. This is not the time to rationalize, justify or mitigate the bad behavior of another, just to say you have forgiven them. Allow permission to be angry at them and eventually at yourself.

In foregoing this step and forgiving someone too early, you are sealing in your own unexpressed and unresolved emotionality, because the extending of forgiveness ends the discussion by closing the door on the past. By not allowing yourself to fully vent all of your negative emotionality before you rush into forgiveness, you begin to limit your capacity to access all of your heart and soul. Sometimes I think we just want to claim we have forgiven someone because it is like some kind of panacea on our road to spiritual enlightenment.

When we take the time to do our own emotional work, we can then see who we really need to forgive and why. What I found in dealing with my own trauma was that I too forgave everybody with the traditional shallow version of "forgiveness lite". I did not know this until I was confronted with the emotional purging during my father's death which caused me to take another look at those persons whom I had already forgiven. There was indeed negative emotionality running underneath the forgiveness I had already offered. Although I did not "take back the forgiveness", I was made aware of just how many levels "total forgiveness" really has.

Instead of trying to force myself to forgive others at a deeper level during situations of crisis, I pulled my attention away from them completely to focus on my own authentic emotionality. I allowed myself in private to own up to how I really felt about the situations I had found myself in. As I processed through my own emotions allowing myself to truly feel the rage, anger, frustration, shame, guilt and sadness, I then realized what was really going on.

I found that the reason I was very upset with others was because I was projecting all of my negative emotionality onto them, in particular my guilt and my shame. As I continued work on myself, I eventually found the root cause of my anger. Behind the trauma and behind the drama of my life, I was most angry at myself because I "abdicated responsibility" for myself, setting myself up for involvement in too many crisis situations.

One of the obstacles to forgiveness is our need to project out the anger onto others as opposed to resolving it within ourselves. Why do I continuously say "anger is projected"? Most agree that people can do things to make you angry. Actually, people do "not" do things to make you angry, people just do things.

The reaction of anger is within you because you are being triggered by their behavior. The anger is your part, the behavior is theirs. It is your thought process giving definition and assigning negative meaning to what they are doing. Your reaction is based upon your own experience, standards and unresolved emotionality which sets off the triggers. Another person in the identical situation could have a completely different reaction.

When I finally stopped projecting my anger onto others and got completely honest with myself about owning my contribution to the chaos then I could begin the process of being completely honest with others. What I realized was the problems I faced were "not all their fault", as I had been claiming. So after forgiving myself, I was finally able to offer true forgiveness to others for their part in the confusion.

Seeing My Reflection

Let me share a story on my difficult road to total forgiveness in a professional relationship. When I was running my consultant business, I talked about having a major contract that allowed me to invoice my client approximately $70,000 per month. Yeah…Per month! There are a lot of opportunities to pursue many personal pleasures with access to that kind of money.

But as I soon found out with that kind of money, one's ego can quickly get out of control. Without my realizing it, my ego and everybody else's egos were running amuck as this project got quickly out of control when the dollars started flowing. After almost a year and a half of this "entitlement mentality" around money, I decided to walk away from this contract.

I ended the contract early, giving myself time to reflect on what had just happened. I always believed money was a good thing which brought prosperity and abundance. In addition, I felt all I needed for my own security was more of it. Now I had all of the money I could ever want but felt completely stressed because of the demands of others that I give them more of "my money".

As you can see from my language, my ego's footprints were all over this situation. I was the one deciding who would get what, when, and how. Of course, this way of making decisions created total conflict. I did not see my contribution to the chaos; until, I stepped away from the contract. I was so angry at everyone who worked with me because of their greed around money, especially the subcontractor.

Once the budget had been set, legal contracts signed and the project ran smoothly for one year before the subcontractor decided to hold the project hostage unless more money was allocated to her company. What angered me beyond belief is how the client directed me to renegotiate the terms with the subcontractor in order to keep the project on schedule. Never mind that it was not fair. Never mind that a legal contract was already in place. How could this be happening to me when I thought I was fair with everyone?

I sat with myself in the quiet, allowing myself to feel the rage and hostility welling up from my unexpressed emotionality. As those negative emotions subsided, I began to feel calm enough to finally look at my contribution to the chaos. I also finally answered the question, "What belief was I holding that made this situation possible"? When I got to see my reflection in the stillness that was my life, I was horrified by what I found within myself.

My darkness was on total display. Just like everybody else in the contract, "my greed" was very present. I never asked anybody what they needed or wanted when it came to negotiating their monetary worth. As the prime contractor, I was the one making "all" of the financial decisions from my ego-centric viewpoint, because I was the one responsible for the billing, reporting and management of the $2 million contract.

I held firm to my way of doing business throughout the contract, never thinking that my attitude was contributing to the conflict. In hindsight, when I finally got this, I just laughed out loud as I thanked those "contentious souls" on the contract, for being my best teachers, showing me unhealed aspects of myself. In our quiet moments, when we finally take the time to look at ourselves, we will begin to realize that our "true human self" is not synonymous with our "innocent self".

Universe Tests Level of Total Forgiveness

Since I had now been able to see my contribution to the chaos in this professional situation, I was now in a position to bring forth forgiveness to the subcontractor who I perceived had hurt me the most by creating unnecessary financial strife in my life. As time goes by, we forget about the conflicts or situations that we experienced, as they start to take a backseat to our ever changing reality.

With this new understanding of the role I played, the memories began to fade and the emotions no longer easily triggered. Over time, I completely forgot about the situation that caused me so much stress. Weeks turned into months and months turned into years, as this memory continued to fade until one day, the universe decided to test my level of "total forgiveness".

I was given the opportunity to do a short-term consulting contract. I found myself flying in and out of town, creating the framework for the assessment I was conducting. You can imagine my surprise when we got to the part where we talked about computer systems, and I found the name of my former subcontractor as one of the companies recommended for this project.

The decision I had to make involved evaluating three separate computer systems in order to pick only one thereby consolidating the agency's computer systems. Hum… you could say the universe has a very interesting sense of humor! I am to be the one who decides if the subcontractor who created the most financial stress for me is the one I would recommend for this project. All I could think about was "what comes around, goes around".

What would you do? If you had the opportunity to decide the future of someone whose actions helped push you into the "financial shark tank", which years later you were still trying to recover from; what decision would you make? My divine impulse helped me make the decision fairly quickly.

In the final analysis, without any emotionality, I picked the computer system my former subcontractor had created, as being the best system available for the project. As you read this, I can hear you saying, "You did what"! Yes, I picked the former subcontractor. When you truly heal your own emotionality and bring forward total forgiveness, it is effortless to "help the one who hurt you".

Word spread quickly to the former subcontractor that I was the one who recommended her computer software. Even though we had not spoken in several years due to the dysfunctionality of our working relationship, I received a call from the former subcontractor wanting to "thank me" for recommending her company. This was a good opportunity for me to provide closure to our old relationship.

I took advantage of the call to ask forgiveness of her for all of the ways in which I created stress for her, by not including her concerns in my decision-making. This apology allowed her to offer her apologies for "not being the easiest person in the world to work with". We both laughed. As I hung up the telephone, I felt the conflict between us had truly been resolved, at a deep soul level; and, no undercurrents remained that created separation one from another.

Many of us believe we have brought "total forgiveness" to those we perceived had hurt us; but, if asked was harmony restored in the relationship, most will say "no". To measure the level of your success in bringing total forgiveness to others, just look at the current nature of the relationship and your willingness to interact with the offending party. If you say you have forgiven, but you are "unwilling" or unable to engage the other, know that your forgiveness has not gone deep enough. You have more work.

If you find yourself in this place, take advantage of reaching out to the offending party to extend an olive branch during holidays like Christmas because our hearts seem to be more open. By mending the relationship, it does not mean you have an ongoing relationship where you interact regularly with them. But, it does mean you could easily engage the person without any unnecessary resentment rising within you. Now, that is "total forgiveness".

CHAPTER 14

Leave No Stone Unturned

L ife is not simply an intellectual exercise where you can direct your mind to do something that your heart has no interest in because our power source is really in the heart. In our current way of being, we give too much honor and recognition to our minds as the decision maker. In the new way of being, it is the open heart which has the power to direct the mind in its activities, for this is the only way to ensure the decisions made are optimal and inclusive. Imagine the level of creativity if everything you put your mind to was connected to a heartfelt passion, to make the world a better place.

Open Up Your Heart Space

In resolving our emotional issues to open up our heart space, it is time to leave no stone unturned. How do you know what issues to work on? The answer is simply to follow what your world is showing you about what needs to be healed within you. What does this mean? It means whenever you find yourself angry, agitated, irritated, or stressed out by the behavior of someone else, then this is the area to turn your attention to.

Honestly feel the feelings within then ask yourself, "Why am I so upset about this"? Try to resist the temptation to simply blame the other person's behavior for we now know it is not the "primary cause" of your upset. Remember, you are trying to operate from a new way of being that requires you to take full responsibility for your own emotional reactions.

Once you answer the first question then ask yourself, "Where has this happened to me before"? In life you will find there are certain patterns of beliefs we hold based upon our experiences. Overtime these beliefs harden into rigid rules of behavior that you follow often requiring others to follow as well when interacting with you. When people violate your unspoken rules, it creates anger or irritation for you. If you continue to enforce this belief, you will soon recognize there is a pattern to the rules that are continuously broken.

Focus your attention on this aspect because some belief you are holding may be limiting you in some way. The "dark angels" you seem prone to engage in conflict with, are just showing you this. It is not that easy to stop the limiting beliefs from dominating your behavior because those beliefs are undergirded by human emotion. To move yourself into oneness with God, self and others you must heal your heart from within.

Compassion is Like Breathing

Let's look at this new way of being to see how the divine self would deal with the subject of compassion. There is no way to observe anything and not feel an instant connection to everything, so compassion is like breathing. When it comes to the behavior of others, when you are operating from your divine self, you are not likely to judge the behavior of others.

This does not mean you do not recognize the "bad behavior" of others as causing disruptions. What it does mean is that even though you see the disruptive behavior, you do not judge it; instead you seek to understand where the distortion lies in the perception of the doer. For all bad behavior is a result of some distortion in the mind which allows the person to see themselves as a "separate self" therefore willing to do things to others that create hurt, harm or danger.

Once you can see the reason for the distortions, then you can bring your compassionate heart to the situation. In our current reality, many of us easily show compassion to those who have been victimized, but believe the victimizers do not deserve our compassion. In the new way of being,

179

nothing could be further from the truth. It is easy to love those who are loveable, but in our divine understanding no one is outside of the love of God. The behavior of someone is not the same thing as the "essential essence" of who God made that person to be.

I know some of you may be asking the question, what about people who murder others or commit violent crimes, are we still to love and care for them as well? In the new way of being, the answer is "Yes". However, the ability to evolve to that level of compassion will never come from your human self, because it is only concerned for itself and will fight to protect the part it perceives as having been wounded by another.

From your divine self you understand you cannot judge the nature of human interactions because you don't know how God is using people in support of spiritual awakening. It is often the most horrible and horrific incidents which offer the greatest opportunities for spiritual growth.

I know this concept of compassion is hard to accept by some of you who might be saying I would think differently if I knew of someone who was murdered. Well, I have had the experience first-hand of being with someone one day only to find out they were murdered soon after. It is a devastating experience for anyone to go through this even once; but, for me I can think of several people I knew who were murdered and "not" because of involvement in crime.

The youngest victim was standing on her front steps talking to her friends when murdered because she was hit by a stray bullet in a drive-by shooting outside of Atlanta. She was a 13 year old honor student in secondary school. In another incident, after work a friend decided to go to a party. While at the party an argument erupted in which he tried to break up a fight, when shots rang out. He was struck by a bullet meant for someone else. Finally, there was a teenage cousin who went back to her hometown for a wedding where she connected with an old friend. When the wedding was over, she never returned, only for family to find out days later that both she and her friend had been shot in the head, while sitting in his car.

I tell you these stories not because I want you to feel badly for me, but for you to know that no matter what has happened in your life, the ability to forgive those who have committed such atrocities, is the only way to elevate yourself to a level of spiritual consciousness. Hatred anchored deep within your heart will never allow your divine self to be at the center of your life. Remember, the goal is to leave no stone unturned, especially the one that conceals your deepest anger and hatred.

Being in the Flow

One of the words that best describes this new way of being is the word synchronicity. In my experience, synchronicity happens when two unrelated events come together at just the right time, providing exactly what was needed when it was needed. Some of us call this "being in the flow" while others may call it pure coincidence; but, what makes this different is, the situation usually benefits you in that moment.

If we could view our lives from God's perspective, we would know beyond a shadow of a doubt there is no such thing as coincidence. While many of us move through life looking for the big events, to signal that "*God is still on the throne*", it is really in the little things where the cause for so much joy can be found.

Let me give you an example of one of my "flow days" which I will call my "Magic Monday". It started with me needing to go to the bank to deposit an unexpected check in the amount of $50. What was synchronistic about this transaction was the check was the exact amount as the money I had taken out of my bank the day before.

After leaving the bank, I smiled to myself as I headed to the post office to renew the post office box for my business. When I arrived at the post office, I brought with me the postal notice stating I needed to pay the charges to keep my box open. I got in a line which moved very swiftly. As I approached the clerk, I informed her of the purpose of my visit. She promptly left the counter and to my surprise when she returned she informed me there was no payment due.

As we were having this conversation, her boss came by; so, I decided to engage him because I had no record on my part which showed I had paid this bill. He went to check on another computer, which didn't take too long. He came back to the counter with the news my post office box had been paid up for one year. I could not believe it. I asked him if it could have been some kind of a mistake with someone else's payment having been misapplied. He said "no" because the box of the other person would have been closed. "Just accept the blessing", the supervisor finally said to me.

My next stop was to the sandwich shop to grab something for lunch. When I arrived there, I spoke to one of the usual cashiers and told him about my good fortune at the bank and post office. He laughed and said I was having a good day so I should continue my winning ways by playing the lottery. I laughed and told him I did not play the lottery, but maybe today I will. As he wrapped my sandwich to go, he then told me he was going to give me a discount because discounts were given to women on Mondays! I laughed out-loud as I said to myself I am really having a "flow day". If this day gets any better, I think I will just orbit!

Since I was feeling really happy, I decided to treat myself to my favorite treat of chocolate covered pretzels, which meant a quick trip to the neighborhood store. When I arrived, I noticed right next door was the gas station where they sold lottery tickets. What the heck, maybe I should play the lottery. I bounced across the parking lot in search of one "scratch-off" lottery ticket for $1. I squealed with delight when I realized I had just won $5. Immediately, I cashed in the ticket at the gas station then proceeded back across the parking lot to buy my chocolate covered pretzels, which now cost me nothing. This was my "Magic Monday". As I headed home reflecting on my day, I realized it is truly the little things in life that create the synchronicity which make life all the sweeter.

When things are going well, we give thanks for our many blessings, but when things are going badly, we question our alignment with God. It is during these times we appear to be "falling out of the flow". I used to think I could stay connected to God simply by focusing my attention on all things spiritual. While I had a degree of success with this type of process, I found it really wore me out trying to control my thoughts to that degree. I kept thinking to myself, there must be a better way of being in oneness with God which does not take so much energy and effort to connect to the creator of all life.

This concept of being in the flow or being one with God was something that truly fascinated me. How can God create us, but yet we are unable to continuously communion with God? In my readings of the Bible and other spiritual books, passages often refer to God *"as being nearer than hands and feet or closer than breathing"*. If this is true, then why did I feel at times so disconnected from God?

Eventually, I came to realize God is "not" in the rituals of religious institutions; instead, God is "within" each of us, as we participate in those rituals. I got to see how I and others have started to use our spiritual rituals as a replacement for true communion with God. God is always available to us, but it is us who have distanced ourselves from God.

In our human arrogance, we believe if we pray or attend church then what we want for ourselves is what God wants for us. When things are going well, many of us do "not" call upon God beyond the rituals or even take the time to thank God in gratitude for what God has already done in our lives. If things are going badly, many of us question God wondering if we have made God "angry" in some way causing us to be knocked out of the flow as we see God through our human lenses.

Rarely do we connect to God for the pure purpose of communion-- not asking, not requesting, not begging but being one with the source of all creation. If we did this from our divine self, we would find God is in the very midst of the activity of our lives, creating perfection beyond our wildest imagination despite our apparent reality.

In this new way of being, we let go of trying to control where our life should be heading, because we are only here to glorify God and perform the work assigned to us to do. This type of connectivity from our divine self does not need any type of ritual to stay strong; so, rituals will recede back into their rightful place, merely as aids, in the process of communing with God. Being clear channels for God's use is what keeps us in the continuous flow.

Our Secrets Are Feeding Our Fears

During this time of spiritual awakening, it will not be so easy to hide your secrets, for in truth, everything will be brought to the light, requiring total honesty from us all. If you think about it, confession is really good for the soul and it serves more than just a ritualistic purpose. If you do not deal with your secrets, they will continue to anchor you to your human-self, delaying your connection to your divine self. Anything you are carrying that creates negative emotionality in your heart space will continue to keep you separate from others; therefore, separate from God.

What is fear? What are we really afraid of? Fear as many of you know, is an acronym which stands for "false evidence appearing real". In order to experience fear you must project yourself into a future situation and anticipate some negative outcome, since fear does "not" exist in the present moment. Fear is always associated with future happenings.

If we could resolve our painful memories and own our secrets, we would stop trying so hard to control the future events of our lives. We would no longer operate from the belief that if we do not control the outcome then we will be somehow worse off. That is why in our human thought process, we have decided we need to take control of the variables in life to ensure we experience what we think we need to. Where is God in this process?

God As Our Decision-Maker

How many times have you gotten what you wished for only to be disappointed? How many times have you "not" gotten what you wanted and felt grateful that was the case? Somehow too many of us have decided by allowing God to truly be the decision-maker in our lives will cause us to have to sacrifice what we truly value. I don't know how this concept got so ingrained in human thinking. For how can you say on one hand that "God is love"; but, then on the other hand refuse to put your trust in God's love. Is the problem we do not "know" God, or is the problem we do not "trust" God?

For me, I had knowledge of God from a philosophical place; but, I did not know God from an experiential place. It was only by releasing my emotional baggage and trusting in divine guidance that I truly opened up my heart space to feel the presence of God in my life. I have enough examples of how God has provided for me when I could not provide for myself. I have enough examples of how God has brought me wisdom that was far beyond my human comprehension. I have enough examples to know God is real for me. If you think about it, I am sure you can say the same thing because God has been at work in your life.

As we join in oneness with God then our personal agenda becomes the same as God's will for our lives. We know beyond a shadow of a doubt God's will for our lives contains a roadmap that is ultimately very good for us. We need to trust God, for the roadmap can only lead to a place where we will experience release from the pull of our human desires. We have to allow our personal agenda to be replaced by "divine impulses", which come out of our communion with God, instead of being sourced by our ego desires.

In order to live without fear, without planning, without goal setting, without controlling or manipulating every variable in the external environment, we must release our ego desires. In essence, our "separate self" will cease to lead, as we truly live out the biblical concept of *"giving no thought to what we shall eat drink or put on"*.

As children of God, we need to remind ourselves we are "not" here for our own edification, but we are here for the glorification of God. As we move into a new spiritual awareness, we must close this gap so we become active participants in God's unfolding plans. I don't know about you; but, I do not believe I have enough information to tell God how things need to be done. It was only in my human arrogance that I thought I did. The more I am learning to trust God, the more wonderful my life is becoming. Where we seek to go, our human mind cannot take us, for our hearts are truly seeking oneness with God who needs to show us the way.

CHAPTER 15

Now is the Time

Now is the time to "anchor a new way of being" in which we give love and compassion to everyone because we see them as an extension of ourselves. Now is the time to join the movement to oneness as we stop living in fear of everything and everyone which seem to carry an element of the unknown.

Now is the time to stop being a "seeker" listening to other people tell you what is best for you instead begin to listen directly to your own internal guidance from God. Now is the time to let go of the "victimization consciousness" where you no longer see yourself as powerless in human dramas. Now is the time to release the need for tying your safety and security to the impermanence of tangible physical reality "tan-phys".

Now is the time to channel your divine impulses from within for the benefit of the whole of humanity instead of just for your own selfish pleasures. In order to experience this new way of being you cannot be halfway in focusing on the values of this world and halfway out focusing on the values of God. Until you are totally ready to join in the oneness, God steps back and waits.

Ego Limits Manifestation

We have to begin rejecting our old way of being which puts our ego at the center of our decision-making. Once you allow your ego to be the decision-maker it limits the flow of intuition because the ego is looking only for certain outcomes. There is a concept in quantum physics known as the "wave of infinite possibilities". This means for every outcome, there is an infinite combination of events which can produce that outcome. However, once your ego focuses your attention on a certain pathway to that outcome, it collapses the "wave of infinite possibilities" into a single set of finite events.

Now, in order for that particular outcome to manifest, all of the events must line up in a certain way to achieve the outcome as outlined. The probability of so many events happening decreases the probability and limits synchronicity while increasing the time it takes to deliver those particular events. If you are operating from the oneness with God, then you no longer are willing to specify the action-steps for the manifestation of the divine impulse. You leave it open to the universe to provide the best solution knowing the best solution will benefit everyone to be affected by the decision including yourself. You know all of your needs are being met because "*God is at work*".

Are You Helping or Serving?

In this new way of being, the need to "help" others is very different from the willingness to "serve" others. You no longer use the arrogance of your ego to decide what someone is in need of or what actions need to be taken. Let's look at these concepts for a moment.

When you "help" someone, your ego is in play because it is deciding, evaluating, and judging what needs to happen in a given situation based on its review of the variables. Because your ego was so involved in your need to help, you end up with a skewed idea of the impact your help will have on another.

You can never know for sure through your own ego if your willingness to help is really help. What this means is someone can ask you to do a certain thing for them which you willingly agreed to do because you foresee this request as being helpful. However down the road you will see by providing the help at that time has now created a level of dependency or incompetence on the part of those you sought to help. It is time to shift our attention away from the "need" to help to allow God to guide our actions through service to others.

In "serving" others, the actions you take are based upon divine impulses sourced from God. Sometimes you are guided to do things for others you do "not" see as particularly helpful in that moment. However as time goes by all things are revealed and you can see how that was exactly the right thing to do. As you learn to serve others you become detached from the outcome and allow for whatever is to be to be.

You no longer push a situation towards a certain resolution. Since you cannot know for sure what it is someone really needs to experience on their spiritual journey, the best thing you can do is not do anything unless you are guided by God. We must be careful here when we talk about serving others.

Due diligence needs to be undertaken to ensure we are "not" operating from our "light shadow self", where we claim God told us to do a certain thing for someone else. The best way to know if your message is truly from God is to check the reaction of the receiving party. If you start to deliver a message then are meet with resistance know that your message is "not" from God. Since the other person is also connected to God they have an intuitive sense of what will be helpful. It is only your ego which is not privy to this level of information.

All of us need to look deeply into our hearts to uncover the true intentions of our actions. Are we trying to help someone because it will bring us accolades and recognition?

Are we trying to help someone in order to escape from feelings of our own inadequacy? Are we trying to help someone because in our arrogance "we know better" than they do?

In order to make the shift from "helping" to "serving" be sure you have healed those "unhealed" parts of yourself that allow your service to come from divine impulses through the filters of your authentic emotionality. You cannot fool God. You cannot pretend to be altruistic if your true intention is self-aggrandizement. Take the time now to find out for yourself what truly motivates your actions. In this new way of being, the goal is to become a clear channel for God's use.

Serving Others Promotes Service to You

It has been my experience on my spiritual journey that when you turn your attention away from yourself not caring who gets the recognition, you begin to project onto the world a new way of being that allows the universe to easily serve you. As you do for others from a pure heart space, then others unexpectedly will do for you. This give and take is not based upon obligation but love. Let me give you a quick example of what I'm talking about.

Just before I sold my house, I was in dire financial straits coming out of a very difficult and costly winter season. Despite my struggles, I decided to answer the call to support a new ministry at my church. I found myself having to use gas money I did not have to travel back and forth to church meetings. I also found myself continuing to contribute to church offerings even though it meant I would have less to eat that day. I knew deep in my heart what I was committed to doing was a service for God that allowed my skills and talents to be of use. Never once did I think I should "not" contribute my service because of a lack of funds.

One Sunday I had to get up really early to present the international missions program to both services at our church. I was really tired because I had many prospective homebuyers in and out of my house for several weeks. I really missed the quiet and calm. After my presentation at church, I received really good feedback and lots of support to serve those less fortunate in other countries. That afternoon when I got home all I wanted to do was sleep. I had not been home long before my real estate agent called and said there was a bid on the house. In serving others, I completely took the attention off of the sale of the house and now the house was sold.

The flow continued into the next day as I was surprised by the good deeds others were doing for me. One of my sisters called and said she had a few dollars to give to me and brought it by. I was chatting with my mailman as he dropped my mail in the box. I told him of my dilemma about the non-working floodlights on the driveway. He put his mailbag down, went across the street to borrow a ladder, then climbed 15 feet up to fix the floodlights on the side of my house.

As the day progressed and since the weather was nice, I decided to "weed and rake the front yard". No sooner had I finished when another neighbor came up the street and offered to help me clean everything up. This was really a wonderful day of feeling supported by others with no effort on my part. None of this happened because I started my day with "focusing my intentions" or in "prayer of supplication asking God for certain things".

Needs Effortlessly Met

In this new way of being you must know for sure your needs will be effortlessly met as you seek to meet the needs of others. You will feel loved as you seek to share the love with others. You will feel supported as you seek to support others. On our current spiritual path too many leaders are focusing much attention on setting your intentions, envisioning your goals and proceeding with action steps. If you think about it, this old way of being which focuses so much on you cannot be the road to oneness. The way to oneness requires you be in right relationship with others.

Since much of our time is spent under the guidance of our egos, we do not often get the opportunity to provide service to others for the pure joy of it all. Our egos will not allow us to support others without a corresponding benefit to ourselves. That is why the new way of being will require you to transcend your ego to experience the "mind of God".

For it is only from this place of universal mind that all information is shared and messages delivered which lead to spontaneous right actions.

In this new way of being, it no longer feels appropriate to use God for your individual glory. You wake up every day feeling blessed because of having made the decision to join your will with God's will. Instead of setting your intentions at the start of your day, you wake up asking God "how can I serve?" This takes the focus off of your needs, wants, and desires which allows you to be an instrument for God's use. As my friend recently stated, "we can now let go of our goal oriented spirituality".

Many are probably wondering "How can you live life if you are no longer setting goals or taking action steps"? The answer is under God's guidance you will feel "compelled" and "propelled" by divine impulses to do certain things requiring your unique skills and talents. There is no longer a need for your personal goals and visions for you know not why you create them in the first place, other than for your personal pleasure. With God as your guide, every action you take is now purposeful.

In this new way of being, you will find you will interact differently with others. It is from your divine self that you are now able to show love, compassion, tolerance, and patience for a "young soul's obsession with arrogance and insensitivity". Because you are now content to be where you are, what you are, and who you are, you no longer wish for, hope for or want to be someplace else. How can there be a better feeling than existing in the love and oneness with God?

As you fully join your will with God's will, you will not hold anyone in bondage to their past bad decisions or behaviors. You understand the pursuit of personal pleasure leads to destructive decisions which can have a negative impact on others. You also understand the laws of karma and that the universe demands equilibrium; so it is "not" your right to bring correction to another soul. Your only response is to be loving and compassionate as a clear channel for God's use. Hold the light in the darkest of situations.

However, if you continue to operate from unhealed emotions, you will contribute to the expansion of the darkness instead of bringing the light. There is no way to continuously anchor the higher emotional vibrations of love, compassion, tolerance, and patience without first healing your own heart. For "oneness" is not simply a philosophy, it is a way of being where you elevate the needs of another person as equal to your own.

In our human way of being, we see ourselves as separate from one another but in our divine way of being we know that is not true. We are all God's children created in his likeness and image sharing the same needs and desires. This is not the time nor is this the place where we can live in the world without concern for one another. We must step up and support a common vision of a world where everyone contributes their unique talents and abilities without thought to race, gender, or nationality.

We must share a common vision where love is freely given and received which makes no one a stranger. In order to have such a world where it is our divine right to be happy, joyful, and abundant then we need to begin to live our spiritual philosophy not just talk about it. If you do not change your ways, you continue to give your ego room to hide while you let it disturb your piece of mind as it seeks justification for attack upon another. In this way, you are perpetuating the very darkness you profess you want to escape.

New Perspective on Giving vs. Receiving

Let's discuss a new perspective on "giving vs. receiving". In our human way of seeing reality we believe "to give" something is the same as "losing something". This perspective is totally true in a world that values "stuff". It is funny to me how we get so attached to our "stuff", yet if it was so valuable then why can't we take our "stuff" with us when we die. It is our human value system that places more importance on the "impermanence of tangible physical reality" than on the "permanence of the infinite invisible".

Ironically, everything that exists every building, every car, every house, every piece of clothing, was first an idea in the mind of its maker. The idea for creation of physical reality came out of the "infinite invisible". If we continue to focus and to fight over the results of creation, we will never have peace. Instead we must shift our attention to the knowledge that God is unlimited and can create through each of us everything that is required for our individual being without taking away from someone else. Everything that grows in nature makes room for everything else to grow, why can't we?

As you begin to operate in the oneness you will see the many synchronicities that God provides. If you feel that something has been taken from you, know that it will not be long before that space is filled with something new. Operating in the oneness with God you will also see that giving and receiving happen simultaneously. You experience great joy in giving anything tangible or invisible because you see another as an extension of yourself. In this way you cannot lose anything because it is shared with another. This inability to share is an indication that you are under the guidance of your ego and therefore more work needs to be done.

When you begin to operate in this new way of being, it can sometimes be a shock to others since many people are still operating from a place of concern for themselves. In the following example is a case in point about how this new way of being operates. As was mentioned before, I was in a process of selling my house when I got a call from the real estate agent that there was a bid placed on the house. Although I was tired I met with the agent as she went through 47 pages of paperwork associated with the sale of the house.

As we continued to talk about the prospective new buyers and their demands, I listened attentively to all she had to say. I was struck by the fact that the new buyers were a young couple with two children under the age of six. The wife was a homemaker and the husband already a veteran of war. I felt an immediate affinity to this young family and therefore my decision-making included the impact on them.

As we started the negotiation process over the selling price of the house, I found myself defending the position of the new buyers against my own realtor! When she wanted to raise the contributions of the new buyers, I found myself telling her… "You can't do that"… "They are trying"… "We must help them". Taking this position to support the new buyers required that I forgo several thousand dollars in proceeds from the sale of my house.

Despite this apparent loss of income for myself, I felt nothing but joy at having helped this young family buy their first house. I believe when you are guided by God to be in service to others there is no way for you to lose, even if in the current moment it appears you have lost. Be assured the universe operates on a principle which allows it to maintain equilibrium and what appears to be been taken will surely be restored.

Conclusion

What happens to my life if I don't guide it? Will my life fall apart because I do not set daily intentions, create action steps or repeat daily affirmations? Is there a God that will step in and take control of my life? Or will my life descend into such chaos it is impossible to repair the damage I have created? This is what I set to find out in the spring of 2009. This book outlines some of the events along the journey which have given me a new spiritual awareness.

This journey really started 20 years before with the reading of hundreds of spiritual and psychology books followed by visits to more than 40 countries where various religious traditions are practiced. What surprised me most was that after I obtained a philosophical understanding of spiritual concepts through my study and global travel, I was subjected to another five years of trials and tribulations, before I could begin to talk about being a clear channel for God's use in creating *"earth as it is in heaven"*.

The things that happened to me, I could not have predicted, nor could I have had the wisdom to understand the pruning that was needed to enhance the use of my various skills and talents. I realized on my journey that all of us are truly here for a greater destiny. The vision we tend to hold for ourselves is too small because self-gratification will only take us so far. What became evident to me on my journey to spiritual awareness was I could "not" take myself there. Meaning, my ego could not find the way to "oneness" because in everything I did, I sought the outcome that would benefit "mainly me". With some struggle, I finally came to know there is no "separate self in oneness".

After much soul searching and many roadblocks, I found the only way out was through…through the darkness within. I only wanted to experience the light, the joy, and the good on my spiritual journey. I held onto the belief I could transcend duality by just believing strongly enough in the light. However that proved not to be the case. Never in my wildest imagination would I have thought I would have to descend into the very darkness I was seeking to avoid. How could it be helpful to access the painful and traumatic memories I tried so hard to forget? If anything, I was always taught it was best to leave unpleasant memories alone and let "sleeping dogs lie".

During the intensity of the last five years, many of the beliefs and philosophies I had read about were put to the test. One of the first beliefs to fall was the idea I needed to control all aspects of my life in order to move my life to oneness. At first I just saw small coincidences which made my life a little easier. The more work I did on my emotional self, the more coincidences seem to occur. Soon I realized the coincidences were being orchestrated by God for my benefit as part of synchronicity which comes with spiritual alignment.

I soon lost some of my resistance to watching my world fall apart, as I let go of another cherished belief which was that my transition to oneness with God would be easy. As

I look back now, it took a lot of courage to do what I did, putting my financial livelihood at risk, especially when I did not have an understanding of "who and what" God was to me. In life we must take risks in order to test our spiritual belief systems, to ensure they are being molded according to God's will for our lives. If we never venture out and follow the divine guidance we are being given, we will never know our true divine destiny here on earth.

I don't know when I absorbed the belief that if I do not plan, schedule, guide, organize or manipulate my life, it will somehow fall apart. In many ways that is true because it happened to me. However, I came to a deeper understanding as things in my life which fell apart were things that no longer served me. When you see it from that perspective, it is easy to realize "nothing of value" is being sacrificed, when you take on the challenge to follow God.

In the end, it is the spiritual journey which changes your human value system. What was once thought of as unthinkable, I learned not to pay much attention to. For instance, it never would have crossed my mind to sell my gold and diamond jewelry I had purchased in Israel and Egypt, believing at that time that everything I had purchased would be mine indefinitely.

So, to be guided to separate from something I "truly valued" required me to alter my belief system enough to allow for the sale of the jewelry to be possible. Once the jewelry sale was completed and the money used to pay property taxes, I was glad to trade one asset for another. To my surprise, I also felt a level of relief because I no longer feared my high-end jewelry would be stolen. For this transition from what is valuable according to my human perspective to what is valuable according to my divine perspective was a fascinating journey. It required that I be spiritually obedient, not allowing myself to waiver, even if the divine message I received was "not" to my liking.

What happens to my life if I don't guide it? As time went on, I found I began to be confused about what was "good" and what was "bad". As my value system changed, it became more and more difficult to analyze and judge situations. Without the ability to provide analysis, it created great difficulty for my ego to function since it only processes information in that way. At one point, I felt I was being split into two. My spiritual philosophy was not fully integrated; so, my human self was trying to use my new spiritual philosophy to manipulate divine power for personal gain. Most of us have been taught to connect to God for the purpose of obtaining some personal desire. I was no different in holding that belief.

The further along I got into the spiritual journey, the more difficult it became to use divine power for my personal benefit because I was weakening my ego structure. This created my inability to live by either my human self or divine self. I was unable to use my mind to control situations happening in my external environment; but, I had not yet become completely one with my divine self. In many ways, I was beginning to feel like a "ghost" in this dimension of reality, because I was able to see things and hear things but unable to affect change. This made me even more concerned because I had caught myself up in a process I had no way of getting myself out of.

The only way out was through and at this point I could not determine which way was through. After several years of going through this process, the anxiety that finally overtook me in this stage was unbelievable. I found myself falling asleep regularly dreaming I was falling off of a cliff. The dreams were so real I would awaken in the middle of the night crying out for God to help me. Night after night for months on end, I was unable to sleep because of this feeling of falling. As I continued to take down the world I created by dissolving my business, closing my office, selling my car, selling my house and spending more quiet time communing with God, this feeling of falling in my dreams began to fade away.

I truly believed as has been said before, my transition from my human self to my divine self was supposed to be effortless. Nothing could have been further from the truth. For all of you on your own spiritual journey please know the road can be difficult; but, if you can stay the course and do what is required to alter your value system, you will eventually come to find God anchored in the center of your world. Make no mistake, God is worth the effort.

On this spiritual journey, I was surprised to find that before I could move into my divine self, I would have to dissolve much of my human self which was creating a separate existence from God. Dissolving my human self would require I spend time in the "darkness within", resolving the painful memories and letting go of my personal agenda which had guided my life up to that point.

All of my readings often emphasized the positive outcomes of spiritual alignment but very few of my readings prepared me for the cataclysmic shift that awaited me. When you are going through something in life, sometimes it is really hard to get the type of support you think you deserve because no-one is experiencing a situation in exactly the same way as you are. So there are times on the spiritual journey, when you will feel intensely lonely. This I believe is purposefully done by God to make us more dependent on God than we are on each other. For only under God's control can our divine destiny be fulfilled.

One of the things that make the journey to spiritual awakening so difficult is that you are required to create "pauses" in time, between the messages you get and any actions you take. In our normal way of being the exact opposite is true. We take action immediately upon hearing messages from our ego minds. It does not matter if our external reality appears to be in sync with what it is we want. Our human way of seeing reality dictates we move ahead in isolation, expecting everything else to conform to our desires. However in operating from your divine self, you begin to see your connectivity to everything; therefore, you willingly wait to proceed until you can see an opportunity for manifestation of the message which confirms the right time to link to the next step.

Our divine way of seeing reality dictates we move as part of the collective and not before. This is a hard concept to actualize because it goes against all of the chatter in our minds. While I was being still and sitting on "pause", my ego mind was telling me to get busy and take actions. Since I resisted my ego's demands, it began internal chatter about my being lazy, self-absorbed and detached from reality. This started to cut into my sense of purpose as my self-esteem began to plummet. Ironically, this drop in self-esteem is what allowed for a little bit of daylight between my ego and my divine self, allowing me to realize I was not this personality.

As I continued to stand up to my ego, resisting the temptation to move before I received a divine impulse compelling me into action, my ego began to change its tactics. My ego became a chameleon. As I became more spiritual, it was as if my ego said "I can do that"! It quickly jumped on board with spiritual concepts just to hijack the process. My "spiritualized ego" was now guiding and directing my actions with regards to building a new business based on spiritual concepts. How many people, especially clergy are currently out there being guided by their "spiritualized egos" while feeling they are fulfilling their divine destiny?

The only way I came to understand my spiritualized ego had hijacked the process was because, everything I did especially those things I thought were "good", never manifested in their fullness. My first spiritual book was channeled by my spirit, but the process of distribution was hijacked by my ego. I had delusions of grandeur that my book would be a bestseller and everyone would be seeking my opinion on spiritual matters. Not only did that "not" happen, but the business which had been hijacked by my ego was soon enough dismantled.

At this point in my process of spiritual awakening, I was very discouraged because I couldn't seem to find my way. What I thought I knew I did not know. I was completely unable to get comfortable with uncertainty. What used to work no longer worked. What am I supposed to do now? How am I supposed to live? Is there really a God? I had way more questions than I had answers. In looking for what I was missing, I reached for a book by Joel Goldsmith entitled "The Thunder of Silence". Since my life was very stagnant I found myself very open to what I was reading.

For the first time, I began to see the disconnection between me and God. Like most people I was seeking a connection to God to access the power of God for my personal benefit. It never dawned on me that God had an agenda for my life that would bring divine power through me but not give it to me. In my daily prayer and meditation sessions, I assured God I wanted nothing more than to be in the oneness. I did not know what this would look like but I was open to finding out.

My desires for the tangible things that made life comfortable were slowly falling away to the point where I had to sell my luxury car and my suburban home, in order to stay on my spiritual journey to find oneness with God. You know you are close to being in oneness with God when you are willing to put on the altar those things you hold dear, for "*where your treasure is, there your heart is also*". When you are willing to sacrifice your human way of life for God, you send the message to the universe, nothing is more important than being "one with God".

Warning, do not try to fool God by offering sacrifices you really don't want to make because God will truly take certain things, in order to "prune" you for use. Most of us want to be close to God when it is convenient for us; but, we do not want to "completely sacrifice" our way of being. Remember, Jesus said to his disciples "*give up everything and follow me*". There is no exception to this rule for the honest seekers of spiritual awareness. The question for you is, "What are you really willing to give up"? Are you truly ready to live in such a way as "*nothing of value can the world give and therefore nothing of value can the world take away*"?

One of the things which continued to give me strength on this spiritual journey was watching my friends and family implement with astonishing results, some of these same spiritual truths. To come out of my own process long enough to hear their concerns and accomplishments, gave me strength to continue on my journey to oneness with God. Because I hung in there with the process, the biggest blessing was the manifestation of a spiritual life coaching program called "ETA 2 Oneness", the details of which you have just read in each section of this book. Never in my wildest imagination would I have thought to create such a program. I feel this program was manifested by God in a similar fashion to the way a musician receives a new song from the divine. My role was only to prepare myself through study, training and global travel for the divine destiny which awaited me.

You have read my story and understand my spiritual philosophy so let's take a moment to talk about your journey. Based upon your own experiences, you too have come to expect certain beliefs will allow you to join the movement to oneness with God. What I would like to do here is share from my perspective, what I consider some of the realities and myths associated with the journey to spiritual awakening as we all try to "anchor a new way of being".

Realities of Spiritual Awakening

Know "Who" and "What" God is to You

One of the foundations of spiritual awakening is to have a clear understanding of "who" and "what" God is to you. Is God to you a "Santa Claus God" here to help you manifest your personal desires? Or is your concept that God is a "Punishing God" waiting to pounce on you because of your missteps? Do you truly trust God not just philosophically but experientially? If you do "not" trust God, it is because you have an erroneous conception of "who" and "what" God is. According to the New Testament, God is portrayed by Jesus Christ as the source of "unconditional love". Who can say unconditional love is not something they are truly seeking? It is this desire for unconditional love that is driving all of our personal relationships to the brink, as we make ego demands on one another seeking the type of unconditional love that only God can provide.

As human beings we are often emotionally immature and unable to see beyond our own ego, which is primarily concerned with the impact of everything on itself. From this place we feel "entitled" to everything we want, even things that are not ours. Given this way of looking at the world through the lenses of our ego, there is no way we can truly move ourselves into spiritual alignment. Therefore, as you make the journey to spiritual awakening, you will increasingly have to count on something greater than yourself. For without an understanding of who God is and how God functions in your life, it will be difficult to persevere through the challenges that will surely face you in the transcendence from your human self to your divine self.

Be Your Own Leader

On your spiritual journey, you must be willing to be your own leader. Do not elevate someone else's experiences or beliefs above your own. Do no compare your way of seeing reality as somehow superior or inferior to others. The reason this is so is because each of us has a unique destiny and no two of us are moving in identical directions. Therefore, no one knows with certainty what it is you should be experiencing. If you take the advice of those you perceive as leaders, you are abdicating responsibility for yourself which can only delay your arrival to oneness.

The major thing you can get from spiritual leaders, are the tools and inspiration to support you on your spiritual journey. For spiritual leaders do not know with certainty, the way through the darkness within you. Only you can direct yourself through these dark places. Most of us are seeking someone to lead us because we really do not want to experience our deepest truths. Unfortunately, the journey to spiritual awakening is all about you coming face-to-face with your deepest truth. You can no longer hide from what you have created. You can no longer claim what you are doing is under the guidance of someone else's suggestion. Everyone must be individually accountable for themselves. We can share the journey together but only to a certain point.

Be Willing to Lose What No Longer Serves You

As you continue through your spiritual evolution, you will come to find there are things which you will have to let go of. Some of the things we have collected along the journey, including tangible things such as houses, cars, clothing, jewelry or friendships may have to be relinquished. In many ways, we are prepared to do that, for we know the tangible things of our lives have served us well. We are more used to disposing and discarding of these things because that is how as humans, we have been programmed. We can always get more "stuff".

However, when you are on a spiritual journey, you may be guided by your spirit, to let go of certain things or relationships without the benefit of seeing what will replace it. This uncertainty can engender great fear and anxiety which is why you need to be clear about your commitment to God. All of your relationships need to be given to God for you to be guided in either making changes to the relationship or ending it. You have to be willing to let go of any relationship that is not serving you. We are far too tolerant of being with others who feel it is their duty to belittle us, mistreat us, or try to dictate the direction of our lives. On the spiritual journey, you have to understand by allowing others to affect you in this way you limit your movement into oneness with God.

Unpack Emotional Baggage

It is time to unpack emotional baggage which is holding you back from your spiritual journey. The type of emotional baggage I am referring to comes from the drama and trauma of your life. Make no mistake; we are all "walking wounded". If you live long enough, you have been victimized by the "underbelly of darkness". You can recount from your own life story: physical abuse, sexual abuse, emotional abuse, betrayal, abandonment, intimidation, manipulation or a host of other bad behaviors. All of the negative emotion you have experienced at the hands of others is still unresolved in too many instances causing you to be triggered. These triggers in our lives come from unresolved emotionality which needs to be dealt with. Instead most of us waste time trying to modify the behavior of others in order to control the external environment.

How do you defuse your triggers? First, you have to know they are real, and they are not going away without you resolving the root cause of their existence. In spiritual life coaching, we are guided to look at the fundamental beliefs controlling our behaviors. Unless you have an understanding of why the behavior was created in the first place, you will have difficulty unpacking emotional baggage. There is a reason why we do what we do. The problem is the reason may no longer exist so the behavior has now become obsolete creating more problems than it is resolving. If you do not understand your own behavior, you will have difficulty moving towards your spiritual awakening.

Update Limiting Beliefs

There is much to learn about ourselves and the reasons why we feel it important to hold on to past painful memories. Many of us believe that by remembering we can avoid similar situations in the future. Nothing could be further from the truth. It is precisely because we keep harmful memories in our conscious awareness that we continue to "magnetize" similar situations, through the "law of attraction" which brings to us situations we most often think about even if that is "not" what we want. For example, if you believe "people cannot be trusted" then, you will continue to experience people who cannot be trusted. It is your belief that makes real the condition for anything to manifest in your world. If you are trying to change the belief that people "cannot" be trusted then you need to collect evidence and shift your focus so you accept as real, the idea people "can" be trusted.

When your ego starts to warn you people cannot be trusted, you can point to other situations where that is not true. This way of being with your ego begins to loosen it up to the acceptance of new beliefs and ultimately new behaviors. This process has to continue until you have given enough room from your ego dominating behavior to give way to the anchoring of divine guidance. Guard what you allow into your mind because it can strengthen an unconscious belief. This is one reason why people often caution us to avoid entertainment that is extremely violent in nature because if this way of being seeps into your belief system, it can desensitize you to the harm violence can do.

Speak Your Truth

In the shift to this new way of being, it is important you always speak your truth. We can no longer be afraid of what people will do or how they will react to us when we disagree with them. I have come to accept most people are allowing their ego to be the decision maker; and as a result, decisions will most likely have a negative impact. I don't take it personally because I understand the job of the ego is self-preservation. Therefore, I do not have to get defensive or be triggered by another person's bad behavior. Instead, I chose to immediately confront those who have made a decision which is having a negative impact on me. By speaking my truth about their decision being hurtful to me, I am also being mindful not to trigger them so they become defensive.

I operate from the place that people are "not" conscious of what they are doing to others. I do not confront somebody from a place of hostility or anger but, instead seek to have a discussion from a place of clarification. A simple question might be "Do you really want to take that action because it will have a negative impact on me in the following ways"? Most people, if given a chance, will admit it was "not" their intention to cause harm to you, because the impact of their decision on you never crossed their mind. Remember, communication is a two-way street.

Be Willing to Be Wrong

You have to be willing to be wrong about everything, for it is your human arrogance which is holding you "bondage to the darkness". Your way of seeing reality was created by your ego which limits what you can understand. You only see your "slice of the pie"; so your decision-making process tends to be fragmented. As a rule, the ego tends to disregard anything that does not support its fundamental beliefs about what it is seeing; therefore, the analysis of the evidence by you will be limited. You fail routinely to include other elements of a situation because often you are unaware of these variables. So, why is it so difficult to admit you were wrong?

There is no way to see the totality of anything if you are using your "ego mind" as the filter. This way of seeing is guaranteed to bring you conflict. The only way to see the whole picture is by transcending your human self and allowing your "divine self" to be the decision-maker. Because of human arrogance, most of us think we already know what we know; so when challenged, we become defensive. Why is that? Could it be because in the ego way of seeing reality, there can only be "one right answer", which is the answer "I" possess? On the spiritual journey, we must begin to admit our limitations and build in more tolerance for how others see things. Admitting we are wrong goes a long way in bringing about tolerance for others as they move along on their spiritual journey.

External Verification of Divine Guidance

Once you understand how you communicate with God, it is very important to verify the "divine messages" you are receiving. If you do not verify the divine messages, how do you know if the messages are from God or your "spiritualized ego"? One of the fastest ways to tell the difference is that the messages from God always benefit more than just you. Also, the messages from God are "time sensitive" meaning you are only given information to handle a situation happening in the "now". This process is in direct opposition to the ego which may give information to handle a situation that "may" or "may not" occur six months from now. This planning and controlling of future events is all the province of your ego.

Therefore, one of the best litmus tests of whether the ego is offering guidance is whether the information being given is future oriented, where the ego is seeking to control external reality. If you are connected to the spirit of God, there is no need to control external reality. When God is involved in your decision making, due to synchronicity, you receive the divine impulse to act at the same time you have the opportunity to fulfill its manifestation.

Myths of Spiritual Awakening

Using Life Lessons to Avoid Future Pain

Many of us believe we are really in "Earth School" with our job being to "learn the lessons" put before us. Some of these lessons are very painful as we are confronted with issues such as abuse, betrayal, intimidation, manipulation or abandonment. The conventional school of thought says if we learn these lessons correctly, we can recognize the signs earlier and avoid similar situations in the future. If we do that, we have truly learned our life lessons. Do you agree with this statement? Well, I don't agree. I believe this is one of the major myths of those on a spiritual path. From a life coaching standpoint, difficult life lessons are meant to show us the areas within our self which are in need of healing.

The secret to truly learning the life lesson is in the ability to change the belief which allows for a change in behavior.

The goal of a life lesson is not to master control or manipulation of the external environment because using your mind to control your life's experiences will only take you so far. To permanently resolve the situation, you should allow yourself to go into the pain, to access the root cause of the experience which is often unexpressed emotionally to release the shadow belief. For example, from previous traumas, many of us have self-esteem issues which are anchored in guilt and shame. It is to this emotional baggage life lessons are being targeted triggering us when confronted with the bad behavior of others. There is a way of being in the world which allows you to maintain more equanimity, no matter what is going on in your external environment. To get to that place, take advantage of what your life lessons are showing not to avoid similar situations in the future, but to truly heal yourself from within.

Your Mind Should Lead and Your Heart Will Follow

In order to move into oneness with God, we must move away from the myth that our minds should lead and our hearts will follow. For in reality, it should be the other way around. Our minds are too limited to lead because they are grounded in physical reality which only recognizes external stimulus. It takes information and puts it into a mechanical way of seeing reality, by analyzing duality such as up/down, good/bad, or right/wrong before rendering a decision. This process of duality is the "realm of the ego" and is therefore subject to distortion, when used by humans as the structure for decision-making. It is time to allow ourselves to lead with our hearts, for therein lies the pathway to God. Your mind cannot take you, where your heart does not long to follow.

For this reason, I am not a big proponent of "discipline". Yes, we can control our minds by enforcing discipline, but this guarantees success only to a certain point. If you really want to make a permanent change in your behavior, access your heart to find out what "need" this behavior is satisfying. Once you understand the root cause, you can begin the process of fixing the alignment issues that exist between your mind and your heart. Many of us may find ourselves reluctant to follow our hearts completely because we do not trust where it will lead us. If this is the case for you, I can only recommend you spend more time unpacking your emotional baggage. For trust issues only reside in unhealed emotionality. Know the "feeling nature" as experienced by your heart, is the gateway to God because it allows for the inclusion of others. In order to be a full participant in this spiritual journey, you must be willing to allow your full emotions to be accessible. One must go through the darkness within before one can come into the light of spiritual awareness.

Resisting Negative People

Many of us believe on the spiritual path we must resist "negative people", moving away from those with "lower level vibrations". Nothing could be further from the truth! For when you move away from the negative, you are moving away from the ability to grow and expand your own spiritual consciousness. Negative situations are showing you that you are out of spiritual alignment somewhere. If you continue to avoid negative experiences or people with lower level vibrations then you are artificially surrounding yourself with what you perceive as "good". This artificial incubation allows your ego to thrive from a position of superiority. This way of thinking does not break down your ego but enforces it. The belief that there is something negative is part of dualistic thinking which again belongs to the realm of the ego. The ultimate goal is to transcend the ego and all of duality into the oneness of God where there is no opposite.

So, if you want to grow and evolve, you cannot skip steps by merely deciding you want to eliminate negative things or negative people. The ultimate test is to be in the presence of what you consider "negative" without being triggered by it. For as has been discussed, if you are triggered by the negative in others it means there is still something "unhealed" within you. Those that are showing you the negative or lower level vibrations, do not shun them; but, allow yourself to go into the darkness of your own soul. For the only way out is through, to this there is no exception.

Goodness and Morality Guarantee Oneness

Many of us believe if we are "good and moral" people living by our spiritual beliefs it will be enough to guarantee our oneness with God. Let's look at this concept a little further. There is no debate most of us would prefer to be around people who are good and moral. However, many people are stepping over the darkness within themselves as they strive to present themselves as "*faultless before God*". It is to this that I am speaking because there are no shortcuts to God. Feeling anger and resentment in your heart, yet displaying an external persona of love, is "not" an acceptable path towards oneness with God.

In order to be one with God, we must first be one with each other. We cannot go to God alone, hiding our indiscretions and bad decisions. There is a role for goodness and morality; but, the difference is that both of these things are the results of being in alignment with God, not separate goals to be pursued. You do not have to strive to be good or moral, if you first seek to be one with God.

We Must Envision Our Own Destiny

Many of us spiritual seekers are very much caught up in the visioning process believing we must create a vision for our lives in order to maximize our talents and abilities. We believe our divine destiny is something we actively create. It is up to us to design it for ourselves then ask God to support our deepest desires. Many of the current spiritual teachers advocate a belief system that encourages its followers to envision what they want for their lives and hold that belief regardless of their current reality. Being able to do this type of mental gymnastics will guarantee a certain level of success. However, this way of being will ultimately fail because it still leaves the ego in control of the desire to be fulfilled. With that being the case, we are being locked into the ego structure without even realizing it. If we can get beyond the belief that we are here to simply satisfy ourselves, then our skills and talents can be used in the building of God's kingdom on earth.

In order to use our talents appropriately, we will have to shift our minds from being "tools of creativity" to being "instruments of attunement" receiving divine guidance. We do not have the ability as humans to synthesize all of the variables in the universe to decide what our vision needs to be to satisfy our individual destiny. This task is only delegated to God who sees the totality of all that is. The way to maximize your skills and talents is "not" through your own personal visioning process, but by becoming a clear channel for divine guidance. We have to learn to trust whatever God has in store for our lives. Moving into oneness with God requires we step beyond our "separate self", no longer focusing on what we think we need to satisfy our human desires. You must trust that God working in your life will only create perfection, if left untouched by the distortion from your human filters.

Applying the Concepts of ETA 2 Oneness

You have read my story and understood my spiritual philosophy, now it is time for you to apply the concepts of "ETA 2 Oneness" to your own life. Below, you will find a series of questions designed to help you find out which areas of your life still need more work. This journey to spiritual awakening is not a process you can do alone because your ego structure is so tightly built that unless you have people outside of your thought system to challenge your answers, you will make little progress.

After answering the questions and explaining your answers, find someone who is objective that you trust to discuss your answers. It can be helpful to use someone trained in these matters such as: clergy, spiritual life coach, counselor, or therapist. The goal is to dissolve the ego structure into the oneness of God, allowing the divine self to emerge as the ultimate decision maker in your life. In this way it is possible to join in the movement to oneness with God, self and others.

Readiness for Your Journey

1) Are you ready for the journey to spiritual awakening by carving out quiet time to be in the stillness with the spirit of God?

2) Have you studied the bible and/or other sacred texts to have an understanding of "who and what" God is to you?

3) Do you believe you have the courage to face the "darkness within" accessing painful memories?

4) Are you ready to let go of trying to control your own destiny?

5) Are you part of a community of spiritual believers in which you attend religious services or participate in spiritual group discussions?

6) Do you have access to a spiritual life coach, counselor, therapist or minister who can give you support, but also challenge you in shifting your perception?

7) Do you have the courage to set boundaries or even walk away from those you love?

8) Are you willing to clear your vessel so you can become "spiritually obedient"?

9) Can you be okay with "not knowing" the solutions to some of your current problems?

10) Do you have the fortitude to wait on God's guidance no matter what is happening in your external environment?

Embrace Your Authentic Emotionality

1) Are you willing to do the consistent journaling required to release your unexpressed emotionality?

2) Who is the person in your life who has caused you the most stress?

3) Are you currently experiencing a stressful situation with this person?

4) Have you ever had a similar situation to the one which is currently stressing you out?

5) What fundamental belief are you holding that allows you to magnetize this situation to your life?

6) What unexpressed emotions are you holding onto that you wish you should have shared with the person who displayed the "bad behavior"?

7) What is your "contribution to the chaos" in this situation either something you did or something you failed to do?

8) Where have you "abdicated responsibility" for yourself?

9) Do you still need to mend the relationship in some way to eliminate the feelings of resentment towards the person?

10) Are you ready to offer "total forgiveness" to yourself and others?

Trust Divine Guidance

1) Do you believe the spirit of God communicates with you?

2) How do you know if it is the "still small voice of God" or your "spiritualized ego"?

3) Which method works best for you in receiving divine messages: clairvoyant, clairsentient or clairaudient?

4) What is your ritual that allows you to connect to your divine guidance?

5) What is your process for staying connected to divine guidance throughout your day?

6) Are you "spiritually obedient" to divine messages even when you are guided to do what displeases you?

7) Do you believe in "personal sovereignty" allowing everyone the right to follow their own truth?

8) Do you feel obligated to share messages with others whom you believe are heading for trouble?

9) Do you believe everyone has the ability to hear the voice of God as it relates to their own affairs?

10) How do you know if your divine message has been externally verified before you proceed?

Anchor A New Way of Being

1) Are you willing to be an instrument in the building of God's kingdom?

2) Have you unpacked your own emotional baggage in order to become a "clear channel for God's use"?

3) Is there any part of you that wants to use your connection with God to fulfill your own personal agenda?

4) Are you more concerned with the impact of negative decisions on yourself than on others?

5) Is your life full of events that appear to be synchronistic?

6) Are you using your skills and talents to the benefit of more than just yourself?

7) Do you feel you should have control over your divine destiny?

8) Are you able to maintain your equanimity and connection to God in crisis situations?

9) Do you need to control, manage or plan the action steps for future events to manifest your divine destiny?

10) How do you know if you are making decisions from your "divine self" or your "human self"?

It has indeed been my pleasure to support you on your journey to spiritual awakening. Know that as you move swiftly along on your spiritual journey, in time you will truly see that "*all things work together for good for those who love God*". Remember to first embrace your authentic emotionality for that is your true GPS system. Next trust divine guidance, even when you are unsure, for the spiritual journey is not without risks. Finally, anchor a new way of being by believing nothing is more important than being in oneness with God in order to do God's will.

As you move along on your spiritual journey, resist the temptation to see "downturns" in your life as somehow being disconnected from the oneness with God. In most instances, it is only the pruning process you may be experiencing at the moment. From this place you will be moved into spiritual alignment experiencing your greatest potential.

I am blessed to have left a few breadcrumbs from my journey. Hoping I said some things which were helpful as you explore your own pathway to oneness with God. I felt ready to take the journey to spiritual awakening, because I was feeling pulled by something greater than myself. I wish you peace and blessings as you continue on your own journey to spiritual awakening.

Afterword

By Pamela Leigh

I have not written anything since I graduated from college more than 30 years ago. The idea of writing this afterword was very frightening. So what I did was to do my prayers before writing this section; and, now, I feel excited about what I am going to share with you. My name is Pamela Leigh and this is my story...

For 20 years, my life was the "pits"; my apartment was a mess; I was 70 pounds overweight; I couldn't keep a job; I had overcome abusive relationships; I was diagnosed with bi-polar disorder and; my only child was a drug addict. You could say I was severely depressed about the condition of my life. To cope, whenever I was not sleeping, I was eating fast-food and drinking wine or beer. I didn't care about my appearance as the mental health drugs along with the alcohol made me slow and sluggish. I attended therapy sessions hoping this would help me; but to my surprise, after 10 years of therapy, I was no better off. Once again, I fell back into a depression as my life continued to spiral out of control.

One day in 2009, I woke up and said to myself, "I need to change my life"! But, how do I do that? Then, the telephone rang and it was Robin Johnson, spiritual life coach, author of this book and my sister. I told her I wanted to change my life, and wanted to start with my apartment. She responded by saying, "I will be over tomorrow; and we will start by moving your refrigerator, to allow for more space in your kitchen". I was excited; I thought this was a great start.

The next day when Robin arrived at my apartment, she started in the kitchen just as we had discussed. I had an immediate negative reaction when she started to move the small refrigerator. I felt resistance to her moving the refrigerator, for as I told her it had been in that very spot for decades. I felt pained as she moved it. I did not know why I felt like this. So Robin gave me a "homework" assignment to journal about my feelings and to think back on past memories to see if I could find the root cause for my reaction.

The next day I shared that even though I had lived in my apartment for 40 years, the movement of my refrigerator triggered a memory of me being "evicted from my apartment" when I was a college student. This was the basis for the resistance I felt. I had forgotten all about that experience; so it was surprising to me to see how this long buried emotional memory had stayed with me.

Robin continued moving throughout my apartment, making changes as she went. After the kitchen, she moved to my living room. I had the same reaction about her moving things. I couldn't see the benefit to all of these changes. However, by the time she got to my son's room, something within me had shifted. I jumped in and said, "I need to take everything out of this room because my son is never coming back!" Instead, I want to make this my sitting room. As I made these changes in my apartment, I was getting more energy to make other changes in my life.

The next major area I decided to tackle was my weight. As mentioned, I was at least 70 pounds overweight. I joined a local gym and started going regularly with my mother. I added to my gym attendance, my private daily routine which was to dance for 1 ½ hours to Michael Jackson's "Number 1 Hits". Sometimes, I danced twice a day forcing my body to actively move for almost 3 hours per day. I cut back on my fast food intake and started eating more fruits and vegetables. Over the course of a year, I lost 40 pounds. I was starting to feel the change in my life. It was really happening.

To ensure my change was sustainable, I knew I needed to deal with my emotional issues; but, I also knew therapy did not work for me. I talked Robin into letting me be her first "case study" for a new program she was developing called "ETA 2 Oneness". Let me briefly tell you how this program helped me. As you know from reading this book, "ETA 2 Oneness" is about moving yourself into oneness with God, self and others. However, it is sometimes difficult to see your own faults and failures, which is why it was helpful to have a spiritual life coach.

As I started the process, I had to learn how to "embrace my authentic emotionality". In doing this, it helped me to create a new belief system by which I could now live a new life. I made the decision to "trust divine guidance" because following my own human guidance left my life a wreck. It did not take long at all before I saw that following divine guidance always allowed for the optimal outcome for all parties and situations. What was a little more difficult to implement was "anchoring a new way of being"; but, every time I made a change, I had more faith that God was guiding me. Eventually, my whole life turned around which helped me believe that I was now living this "new way of being" with God at the center of my life and my divine self the new decision maker.

By using the ETA 2 Oneness technique called "homework", I began to feel the emotional changes in me at the deepest levels. Every time I did my "homework", there was a change. The issues to be worked out were identified based on conflict that had come up in my current environment. As I write this afterword, I have now done major rehab on my apartment opening up the space to the point where it feels like a new place. I have lost 40 pounds and kept it off since I implemented lifestyle changes and not simply diet techniques. I am a regular at the gym. I also rejoined my church community.

Additional changes include taking only a fraction of the mental health drugs, focusing mainly on those drugs that keep the chemical balance in my brain. I no longer drink every day, but instead on holidays and special occasions. I am past grieving my son's life; accepting what has happened to him and owning my "contribution to the chaos" that is his life. I now pray to God for His will to be done in my son.

I am no longer depressed in anyway as my relationship with my family and friends is wonderful. I accept them for who they are and I don't want to change them. As for a job, being one of the first case studies for ETA 2 Oneness has allowed me to support my younger sister in her insurance agency.

I have found peace and joy through the ETA 2 Oneness process. I am proof, it works! It assures you of "sustainable change". I used to be a "television junkie" feeling the comfort it provided. Now, after participating in ETA 2 Oneness, "silence" gives me the most comfort, since it allows me to more easily hear my divine messages. Change is all around us, all of the time. If you fear change, you can get lost, as life continues to move. You have to be willing to change to see what happens? You have nothing to lose and everything to gain. Being willing to change, has left me in a wonderful place. I never would have imagined all of the "good" that has come into my life.

Suggested Readings

ACIMI, *A Course in Miracles*, Barnes & Noble, Inc. China 2007

Braden, Gregg, *The Spontaneous Healing of Belief*, Hay House Inc., New York, NY 2008

Dyer, Wayne, Ph.D., *There's a Spiritual Solution to Every Problem*, HarperCollins, New York, NY 2001

Dyer, Wayne, Ph.D., *Excuses Begone!: How to Change Lifelong, Self-Defeating Thinking Habits*, Hay House Inc., New York, NY 2009

Ford, Debbie, *Courage: Igniting Self Confidence*, HarperCollins New York, NY 2012

Ford, Debbie, *The Dark Side of the Light Chasers*, Riverhead Books (Division of Penguin Putnam) New York, NY 1998

Goldsmith, Joel, *The Thunder of Silence*, HarperCollins, San Francisco, CA 1961

Goldsmith, Joel, *Practicing the Presence: The Inspirational Guide to Regaining Meaning and a Sense of Purpose in Life*, HarperCollins, San Francisco, CA 1986

Green, Adele, Can You See Me Naked: Grow in a Conscious Relationship, Life Philosophy, Johannesburg, South Africa 2013

Hay, Louise, *You Can Heal Your Life*, Hay House Inc., Carlsbad, CA 1984

Hicks, Esther and Jerry, *Ask and It Is Given: Learning to Manifest Your Desires*, Hay House, Carlsbad, CA 2004

Jakes, T.D., *Instinct: The Power to Unleash Your Inborn Drive*, Faith Words (Hachette Book Group), New York, NY 2014

Johnson, Robin, *Awakening of a Chocolate Mystic*, Balboa Press (Division of Hay House), Bloomington, IN 2011

Moses, Jeffrey, *Oneness: Great Principles Shared by All Religions*, Ballantine Books, New York, NY 2002

Meyer, Joyce, *Battlefield of the Mind: Winning the Battlefield in Your Mind*, Warner Books Inc., New York, NY 2002

Meyer, Joyce, *Change Your Words Change Your Life: Understanding the Power of Every Word You Speak*, Faith Words (Hachette Book Group), New York, NY 2013

Osteen, Joel, *Break Out!: 5 Keys To Go Beyond Your Barriers and Live and Extraordinary Life*, Faith Words (Hachette Book Group), New York, NY 2013

Tolle, Eckhart, *A New Earth: Awakening to Your Life's Purpose*, Button (Penguin Group), New York, NY 2005

Vanzant, Iyanla, *Peace from Broken Pieces: How to Get Through What You're Going Through*, Hay House Inc., New York, NY 2010

Reader's Guide
Book Club Discussion

1. The author opens the introduction to the book with some thought provoking questions. Have you ever pondered the following ideas?

   "What happens to my life if I don't guide it? Will my life fall apart because I do not set daily intentions, create action steps, or repeat daily affirmations? Is there really a God that will step in and take control if I completely let go?"

2. How do we get beyond speaking about spiritual philosophy to consistently living our spiritual beliefs resulting in "oneness" with God, self and others?

3. What seems to be the biggest obstacle to minimizing the "I don't care attitude" when it comes to the needs of another? How can we better follow sacred text that encourage us to elevate another person's needs as equal to our own, thereby mitigating a potential negative impact on them?

4. The author spends the first part of this book talking about the importance of being authentic. Do you see a connection between the spiritual journey to oneness and the need to embrace your authentic emotionality?

5. Do you agree with the author when she talks about personal responsibility and owning your contribution to the chaos? She states:

"If we do not deal with our "contribution to the chaos" we continue to focus our anger on what someone else did to us instead of what we have contributed to the situation. We must take personal responsibility for every decision and every situation in which we find ourselves, for this is part of the new way of being".

6. What would you do if given the opportunity to "stick it to someone" you thought had harmed you in some way? Would you extend "true forgiveness" to the point of helping the one who hurt you? The author details her experience with forgiving the person most responsible for pushing her into the "financial shark tank" then gave that person another opportunity to make money?

7. Have you ever experienced a "divine impulse" in which you felt compelled or propelled to take some action which proved to be extremely beneficial?

8. How do we get our "ego" out of the driver's seat and stop it from creating separation and conflict as it defends some "earthly value"?

9. Do you agree with the author's assessment of the concept of "forgiveness lite"? In it she states:

   "I would beg to differ with most people who say they have "forgiven" someone with whom they had a difficult relationship, because the offer of forgiveness usually comes "too soon" in the healing process. When we are hurt or when we are in pain, we are in no condition to forgive anybody for anything. The first step in truly learning to forgive is the full self-expression of the pain that is in our own hearts. This is not the time to rationalize, justify or mitigate the bad behavior of another, just to say you have forgiven them."

10. What suggestions do you have to help "anchor a new way of being" where we become obedient to God in the building of God's kingdom on earth?

About the Author

R obin L. Johnson is the Facilitator of ETA 2 Oneness, an organization which uses spiritual life coaching principles to help people move towards oneness by transcending their human self into their divine self. After studying personal and spiritual development as a hobby for 20 years while working as a management consultant, Ms. Johnson recently decided to enroll at the Lutheran Theological Seminary of Philadelphia.

Prior to enrolling in seminary, Ms. Johnson tried to find answers to some of life's most pressing questions such as "Is it really possible to practice tolerance, patience, kindness and love in a world full of violence, anger, hatred and selfishness?" She sought answers through the study of the world's major religious traditions including: Christianity, Judaism, Islam, Taoism, Hinduism and Buddhism. Ms. Johnson integrated her study of religious traditions with travel to 40 countries around the world where these religious traditions are practiced including: Italy, Israel, Egypt, China, India, Thailand and Peru.

Having achieved her version of the "American Dream", Ms. Johnson became more dissatisfied as she felt separated and isolated from God. One day after seeing Debbie Ford, New York Times Bestselling Author on Oprah talking about her concepts, Ms. Johnson soon realized what was missing from her life. It was access to her emotionality which had been tied up with past trauma. Afraid to fully express for fear of what would emerge, she hunkered down in trying to reach God through her mind. As Debbie Ford was fond of saying, the "longest journey is the one from your head to your heart." Ultimately, Ms. Johnson became a certified life coach under Debbie Ford.

Ms. Johnson values education, so in addition to being in the seminary, she has obtained the following degrees: BA, MA, MBA and Certificate in Life Coaching. Currently, Ms. Johnson who resides in suburban Philadelphia is a speaker, author and spiritual life coach.

www.eta2oneness.com